Revive Us
Again!

Revive Us Again!

Realistic thinking on revival

edited by David Matthew

Contributors:
Roger Aubrey, Ivor Hopkins, Bryn Jones,
Keri Jones, David Lazell, Tony Ling,
David Mansell, David Matthew, Wesley Richards,
Alan Scotland, Paul Smith, Hugh Thompson,
Terry Virgo, Arthur Wallis

Harvestime

Published in the United Kingdom by:
Harvestime Services Ltd, 12a North Parade, Bradford
West Yorkshire BD1 3HT

Much of the material in this book originally appeared in
Restoration magazine
This compilation first published by Harvestime
First printed March 1990

Scripture quotations are generally taken from the
New International Version. Copyright © 1978 by the New York
Bible Society and published by Hodder & Stoughton.
Used by permission

Also quoted:
New American Standard Bible (NASB)
King James Version (KJV), Revised Authorised Version (RAV)

British Library Cataloguing in Publication Data:

Revive us again!
  1. Christian church. Revivals
  I. Matthew, David II. Aubrey, Roger
269'.24

ISBN 0-947714-83-9

Typeset in the United Kingdom by:
E. Thompson (Typesetters) Ltd., Bradford BD8 7BX
Printed and bound in the United Kingdom by:
Richard Clay Ltd., Bungay, Suffolk

Contents

'Repent . . . and turn to God, so that your sins may be wiped out, that **times of refreshing** may come from the Lord'

Acts 3:19

Foreword

Several features in this compilation make me glad of the privilege of contributing a foreword. I would mention four in particular.

The first is that it soon becomes obvious to the reader how true is David Matthew's introductory comment that 'the contributors, to a man, are deadly serious about the need for revival'.

These chapters do indeed come from full hearts that have persisted for many years in a deeply-held vision. That is why I welcome their publication. I believe we are at a point where we need an interchange of vision on revival — vision that has its springs in this kind of deep and prayerful conviction.

Today God is creating a fresh vision for revival, and there is a need, right across the Christian spectrum, to hear one another's heart on this matter.

We are sometimes a little too prone to listen more to each other's minds than to each other's hearts. We tend to get defensive (and offensive!) rather than warm and open. It is a time for us to sharpen each other in heartfelt vision for the greater purposes of God, and to that we need to bring bigness of heart, letting go of smaller things.

The second reason is that, though pertinently commenting on the past, these essays have a thread in them which distinctly points us forward, putting revival fairly and squarely in the context of God's end-time purposes.

We are not given only the 'backward look'. We are presented with a panorama of great and mighty outpourings of the Spirit preparing the way for the coming of Jesus. We are in the realms of the 'latter rains' and the final harvesting.

This, it seems to me, hits a note all too often omitted in thinking about revival. The church in Britain has tended to amble along unaware of the extraordinary movements of the Spirit of God across the world in our century. We have failed to perceive the increasing momentum of the harvest ingathering that we are witnessing.

We need to breathe afresh the vision of being in the midst of a mighty flow of God that promises to increase up to the coming of the King.

In this connection there is, in certain parts of the book, a powerful ring of personal revelation in which the glory of God's purposes can be distinctly felt.

It is good to hear from those to whom such revelation has for many years provided an unusual breadth of revival vision. They are men who have understood that times of refreshing from the Lord and the sending of the Christ are inseparably connected in God's thinking (Acts 3:19-21).

A third important feature — which for many may appear somewhat trenchant in presentation — is the persistent reminder that revival is not something that God sends merely to allow us to fill up old and decaying church wineskins. It is not God at work bolstering up our traditions or the status quo.

Revival is not a spiritual face-saver! When God moves in power he will make severe inroads into our biblical understanding and our understanding of structures. He expects us to hear and adapt. Unless we are prepared for that and ready to move in response, we shall miss so much of what God is wanting to do.

It is important to see this clearly because the church has proved persistently slow in responding positively to new insights and new structures. This has been one of the most obvious and distressing features of the history of revivals.

None of us is without blame here, and we all need to be open to God on the issue. Neither is it a fault of nominal believers only. It can, we are reminded, be laid at the door even of those most recently in blessing. Perhaps we need to be jolted into recognising this — even annoyed by radical comment!

On this question, the writers correctly point out that an important aspect of revivals is that they are intended to restore permanently to the church those new insights and structures.

The Moravian revival restored missionary vision. The Pentecostal revival restored a sense of praise, as well as spiritual gifts. But in each case it was nearly a century before the new insight gained wide recognition, and then only after much scorn and opposition.

We ourselves must be ready for God-given restorations of truth to become fully built into our outlook and activities, and passed on to a new generation.

It is to be hoped that the immense importance of this truth will be readily accepted despite the fact that some readers will want to differ in certain details. We should not be so busy straining out a gnat here that we swallow a camel!

The fourth reason for which I am glad to pen this foreword is simply because my own pathway has not been in the 'restorationist' stream.

That enables me to act on my own deeply-held conviction that it is a time for us all to affirm in each other what we know to be God-imparted vision and concern, no matter where we have come from. It is a time for us to let hearts touch, not to be touchy.

It seems to me that if revival means anything, it means approaching one another with a heart as big as God's, with all its patience, tenderness and understanding. It means a melting in the warmth of the love of the cross.

If we mean business for God, and if we are genuinely seeking the day of great revivings, our pathway will be one of increasing response to both truth and love.

Bob Dunnett
Pray for Revival

Introduction

On my first visit to the USA a generous Christian lent me a car to get around.

Left-hand drive was no problem — I had driven in France — but he had to explain the automatic gearbox and the foot-operated 'handbrake'. Thanking him, I gave a cheery wave and drove off down the road.

In spite of its six-litre engine, the car seemed sluggish, and even putting my foot down didn't help much. Then I smelt the smoke. Suddenly, the truth dawned: I was driving with the 'handbrake' on! A quick movement released it. What an amazing difference — the car took off like a drag-racer!

I think revival must be something like that. The everyday progress of the church, slowed down by apathy, tradition, mixture and division, suddenly enjoys a surge of power. As the Holy Spirit releases the brake, barriers come down, God's people glow with life and the lost are gathered into the kingdom in huge numbers. God's purpose goes into turbo mode.

There is a growing wave of concern to see revival in our time. Apart from countless local groups, crowds of thousands are gathering – not for concerts, gospel campaigns or entertainment, but simply to pray for revival. People are reading up about the heady days of Wesley and Whitefield, Moody and Finney, the Welsh Revival of 1904 and the more recent Lewis awakening.

Like a small boy gazing at a bike in a shop window and

coming away determined it will be his, God's people are being
smitten by a holy covetousness. What has taken place in past
revivals, they believe, can happen again. It *will* happen again.
It must!

But dreaming is not enough. The boy has to face the
realities of bike-buying. If the gleaming machine is ever to
be his he must save hard, reduce his chocolate quota, boost
his income by car-washing, and begin to appeal to his dad's
generosity. So with revival. Daydreaming alone will achieve
little, except to sentimentalise the issue.

This book tries to square up to the practicalities of revival.
It looks back to past awakenings, including the build-up to
them, and analyses their characteristics. It looks into Scripture
to find a warrant for future revival on a large scale. Then
it faces the toughest question of all: What can we do now?

Most of the material appeared over several years in the pages
of *Restoration* magazine. The contributors, to a man, are
deadly serious about the need for revival. They pray for it,
weep for it, work for it.

May this book be a help and stimulus to all who share their
concern.

David Matthew
Editor

Part One

Looking back to past revivals

'We can chart our future clearly and wisely only when we know the path which has led to the present'

Adlai Stevenson

Patterns in the build-up to revival

Wesley Richards

The many documented revivals of the past provide us with clues as to the imminence of revival still to come

'We are more popular than Jesus Christ'. So said John Lennon in the heyday of Beatlemania.

Those same 'swinging sixties' saw Christianity in Britain reeling under a prolonged assault of humanism and hedonism. The Pill, pot and permissiveness were in. Biblical morality was out.

Homosexuality and abortion were legalised within one ten-day period in 1967. Divorce was made cheap and easy. Explicit sex and violence dominated the TV screen. Theatre censorship was abolished. God was pronounced dead.

Light in the darkness

Yet today, the British Prime Minister calls for a return to old-fashioned moral values. Christianity is required to be taught more diligently in school. A broadcasting watchdog authority has been set up. The spectre of AIDS has sobered sexual libertines. And over a thousand new churches have been generated in the past fifteen years.

True, permissive legislation still remains firmly in place and ninety-one per cent of the population regularly distance themselves from the churches. But times clearly are changing from what they were a quarter of a century ago.

Sweeping spiritual revival may not yet be taking place, but the signs that one is on the way are remarkably similar to those that have preceded previous powerful visitations of the Holy Spirit.

History, not just biblical promise, clearly shows that it is in the darkest hours that the light of Christ has shone the brightest.

Dark days

The situation in the eighteenth century was, if anything, worse than that today.

Bishop J.C. Ryle wrote: 'From the year 1700 to the year of the French Revolution (1789), England seemed barren of all that is really good. Christianity seemed to lie as one dead. Morality, however much exalted in the pulpits, was thoroughly trampled underfoot in the streets.

'There was darkness in high places and darkness in low places – darkness in the court, the camp, the Parliament, the bar – darkness in the country, and darkness in the town – darkness among the rich and darkness among the poor – a gross, thick, religious and moral darkness – a darkness that might be felt.[1]

Cruelty and materialism

If you think that might be an overstatement, consider these facts: Every sixth house was a gin shop. A familiar sign outside pubs in the 1730s was, 'Drunk for a penny, dead drunk for two pence, straw to lie on'. Gangs of 'drunken ruffians' were said to have paraded the streets and 'subjected women to nameless outrages, and defenceless men to abominable tortures'.

Over a hundred and sixty crimes had the death penalty. Hanging was a daily gala event; those jerking on the ropes were watched and applauded by men, women and children, who crowded the gallows for the best view.

Prisons were unimaginable nightmares: young and old, hard crook and first offender thrown together to fight for survival. Brutal sport included bear- and bull-baiting and cock-fighting. The theatre was the scene of obscenity – 'That sink of all corruption', John Wesley called it. Polygamy, fornication and homosexuality were deemed acceptable.

Materialism pervaded national life. Social unrest attended the enclosure movement, when common land was fenced off, forcing landless workers to move to the cities.

Dead religion

In the cold 'age of reason', God was viewed as an absentee Creator and anything smacking of religious zeal was frowned upon. Six students were expelled from Oxford University because 'they pray and read and expound Scriptures in private houses'.

While the Church of England was still influential – dominating higher education, for instance – it was 'inadequately equipped to face a crisis'.[2]

Nonconformist dissenters, at ease in their newly-found freedom from religious persecution, were fragmented and for the most part spiritually lifeless.

Bishop George Berkley in 1738 wrote despairingly of the 'accumulating torrent of evil which threatens a general inundation and destruction of these realms'.

Moral revolution

Within a year, however, 'all heaven was let loose in Britain'.[3]

Preachers like Wesley and Whitefield burst upon the scene in Britain – spearheading, under God, a huge spiritual transformation, rather than the violent political revolution that later overtook France.

Tens of thousands of unbelievers, in a population of five and a half million, were swept into the kingdom of God. The Methodists alone gained a hundred and forty thousand members.

The power of God was unleashed among huge crowds and many fell to the ground under conviction of sin. Nominal church members were changed into New Testament Christians. Mission activity was launched throughout the world and social justice – abolition of slavery, prison reform, educational and medical care, help for the under-privileged – was given a huge boost.

A century later, W.E.H. Lecky, the free-thinking historian, referred to 'a great moral revolution in England: it planted a fervid and enduring religious sentiment in the midst of the most brutal and most neglected portions of the population, and whatever may have been its vices or defects, it undoubtedly emancipated great numbers from the fear of death and imparted a warmer tone to devotion, and a greater energy to the philanthropy of every denomination both in England and the colonies'.

Pointers to revival

But how did it come about? What led up to it? Did it just happen or were there pointers to revival?

For sure, outpourings of the Holy Spirit, as on the day of Pentecost, are sudden and dramatic. Yet there are clear indications today that the way is being prepared for revival. In such a countdown, the following signs are to be seen:

1. The raising of small 'remnant' groups ahead of time to enable them to prepare the way for others

The *seeds* of revival are sown generations before the *reaping* of revival. Before God works in the masses he prepares the hearts of a faithful few who seem at odds with the faith and practice of other Christians in their generation.

The Moravians were such a group. They were spiritual descendants of Jan Hus – a Czech priest who was martyred in 1415 for his condemnation of a corrupt church and his uncompromising emphasis on personal purity.

In 1722, a small band of Moravians settled on the German country estate of Count Nikolaus von Zinzendorf, who had opened his land to protestant refugees of various persuasions. Here, after a dramatic encounter with the Holy Spirit, 'their hearts were set on fire with new love and faith towards their Saviour and likewise with burning love towards one another'.

From this base, a worldwide missionary enterprise began which brought them into contact with the Wesley brothers, John and Charles.

When John Wesley searched for assurance of saving faith it was to Moravian Peter Bohler that he went for counselling.

A. Skevington Wood writes: 'Many of the features of the Moravian community were taken up by the Methodist societies, for example, the love feast, along with the watch night and the class meeting. Wesley was soon to part company from the London Moravians and take a line of his own, but he owed them an incalculable debt.

'Much of the inspiration for Wesley and Whitefield can be traced back to the Moravians.'[4]

Dr Martyn Lloyd-Jones stresses that God always begins with such small groups, the forerunners, before he does something great: 'If we wait for the whole church to move, it will never happen. Do not worry about that. God's way is to take hold of individuals and to use them and then eventually the majority will be affected.'[5]

2. The parallel emergence in different parts of the country of a small, unofficial band of people whose hearts God has touched

In marked contrast to the official leadership of the day, God raised up a new breed of enthusiasts, whose allegiance was to him alone. Bishop Ryle wrote: 'The men who brought deliverance were a few individuals, most of them clergymen from the established church, whose hearts God touched about the same time in various parts of the country.

'They were not wealthy or highly connected. They had neither money to buy adherence, nor family influence to command attention and respect.

'They were not put forward by any church, party, society or institution. They were simply men whom God stirred up and brought out to do his work, without previous concert, scheme or plan.'[6]

Most of these men, significantly, were young men.

George Whitefield, the son of the proprietors of the Bell Inn, Gloucester, was, at twenty-two years of age, 'declaring the gospel in the pulpits of London with such fervour and power that no church would hold the multitudes that flocked to hear'.[7]

Schoolmaster Howell Harris, son of a farmer, was just twenty-five when he carried out evangelistic work in North Wales comparable to that of the Wesleys in England.

Daniel Rowland was only thirty when people flocked from all over Wales to hear him preach – something he continued to do with 'unparalleled results' from his Llangeitho base for forty-eight years.

Further north, William Grimshaw of Haworth, a complete stranger to Wesley and Whitefield, had been similarly prepared by God. At thirty-four, bereaved of his beloved wife, he was launched into a fervent 'apostolic' ministry, which made a great impact among the 'lower classes' throughout Yorkshire, Lancashire, Cheshire and North Derbyshire.

In Cornwall, thirty-two-year-old Samuel Walker began a far-reaching ministry from Truro and had completed his life's work at the early age of forty-seven.

Wesley was a grand old man of thirty-six, and his brother

Charles just thirty-two, when the eighteenth century Pentecost came in 1739.

3. A renewed search for holiness

Sin becomes an issue before any significant forward move of God's purpose. Nehemiah was aware not only of his own sin but of the sins that God's people, 'including myself and my father's house', had committed (Nehemiah 1:6).

Isaiah cried simply, 'Woe to me! . . . I am ruined! For I am a man of unclean lips, and I live among a people of unclean lips' (Isaiah 6:5).

Similar sentiments were expressed by members of the small but influential Oxford 'Holy Club' to which the Wesleys and Whitefield belonged in their student days.

'Its members,' writes Arnold Dallimore, 'practised early rising and lengthy devotions and strove for a self-discipline which left no moment wasted throughout the day. At nightfall they wrote a diary which enabled them to scrutinise their actions and condemn themselves for any fault.'[8]

Whitefield recalled: 'I joined with them and left no means unused which I thought would lead me nearer to Jesus Christ.'

Though some of their activities were shot through with legalism, they undoubtedly revealed the extent of the deep heart-search for God himself.

4. A drawing together of God's people in a common burden for prayer

Just as a united praying group preceded the day of Pentecost, so did the Moravians' new-found unity pave the way for prolonged intercession.

In 1727, on 25 August, a round-the-clock prayer meeting began which was to last for over one hundred years of continual intercession. Various groups committed themselves to a specific hour for prayer so that at any point of the day or night someone was praying. In the next decade or so, intercessory groups were to spring up in different parts of the country as God drew people aside to pray for a visitation from heaven.

Such intercessory prayer preceding revival often begins in a low-key way. Spurgeon asked: 'Have you ever heard of the great 1858 American Revival? An obscure man laid it up in his heart to pray that God would bless his country.'

That man was Jeremiah Lanphier, newly-appointed city missioner in a down-town New York church. He printed handbills inviting 'merchants, mechanics, clerks, strangers and businessmen generally' to join him in 'calling upon God' at a noonday prayer meeting every Wednesday.

Six came to the first meeting on 23 September 1857. This increased to twenty on the second week and forty by the third week, when it was decided to hold daily lunchtime prayer meetings.

In the next week, news came through of a great revival in Hamilton, Ontario, Canada, and just a week later there was a great financial crash.

As people felt their need for God, prayer meetings became crowded. By the beginning of 1858, the Fulton Street prayer meeting was so crowded that the only way they could accommodate the numbers was by holding three simultaneous prayer meetings in rooms on different floors in the same building.

Colin Whittaker says, 'Prayer became the order of the day. In March, a noon prayer meeting was commenced in a large theatre. Half an hour before the announced time, it was packed out – the great majority being men – businessmen!

'Three days later, the outstanding preacher Henry Ward Beecher led three thousand in that theatre prayer meeting. The newspapers began to sit up and take notice and to report on the happenings. It was front page news that over six thousand were attending daily prayer meetings in New York.

'Other great cities like Boston, Chicago, Washington, Buffalo and Newark soon had their noonday prayer meetings, too. In Washington, five daily prayer meetings were launched, commencing respectively at 6:30 am, 10 am, noon, 5 pm and 7 pm; by April, thousands were attending. It became common sight to see businesses closed with a notice: "Will reopen at the close of the prayer meeting." "[9]

5. A re-emergence of authoritative biblical preaching

In an age of discussion and cool Christian apologetic, the word of the Lord sounded forth with a trumpet blast that woke a nation.

Writes J.C. Ryle: 'They preached simply. They preached fervently and directly. They believed that you must speak from the heart if you wish to speak to the heart. They taught constantly the sufficiency and supremacy of Holy Scripture.

'They taught the total corruption of human nature. They preached that Christ's death upon the cross was the only satisfaction for men's sins, the just for the unjust. They taught constantly the great doctrine of justification by faith. Justification by virtue of church membership, justification without believing or trusting were notions to which they gave no countenance.

'They taught constantly the universal necessity of heart conversion and a new creation by the Holy Spirit. They proclaimed everywhere to the crowds whom they addressed, "You must be born again." They preached the inseparable connection between true faith and personal holiness. No fruits – no grace was the unvarying tender of their preaching.

'They preached God's eternal hatred against sin and God's love towards sinners. Both about heaven and hell they used the utmost plainness of speech. They never shrank from declaring in plainest terms the certainty of God's judgment and of wrath to come if men persisted in unrepentance and unbelief; and yet they never ceased to magnify the riches of God's kindness and compassion and to entreat all sinners to repent and turn to God before it was too late.'[10]

6. A willingness to embrace methods that would work in their generation

Whitefield and the Wesleys were so convinced that, at all costs, the masses must hear the good news of salvation that they were ready for any innovation necessary to get the job done.

As more and more church doors closed to them, they defied convention and took to the open air. They preached in the fields, in the graveyards, in the streets, at fairs, in market-places, even at public hangings.

They would preach anywhere and at any time they could get a hearing. John Wesley's journal reveals that frequently he would preach at five in the morning because that was the most convenient time for factory- and mine-workers to hear him.

'Whitefield and the Wesleys,' writes Bishop Lesley Marsden, 'were called mad enthusiasts because they would free the gospel from the confining Gothic arches of established religion and release it to the masses in street and field, to the sick and unclean in hovel and gutter, to the wretched and condemned in bedlam and prison.'[11]

As an unconventional strategy for reaching the aristocracy, Selina Countess of Huntingdon found a place in her domestic chapels and drawing-rooms for preachers to proclaim the gospel.

7. The bringing together of key leaders for consultation and prayer

Already Whitefield and the Wesleys were being used by God in different spheres – at home and abroad. But at the start of 1739, what Whitefield called 'seven true ministers of Jesus Christ, despised Methodists whom God has brought together', met for a week of discussion and seeking God.

Whitefield recalled: 'Sometimes whole nights were spent in prayer. Often we have been filled with new wine and often we have been overwhelmed with the divine presence.

'On the evening of 1 January 1739 other brothers, about sixty in all, joined them in a love feast where they were moulded together in a great sense of unity and destiny.'

'About three in the morning,' reported John Wesley, 'as we were continuing in prayer, the power of God came mightily upon us. Insomuch that many cried out for exceeding joy and many fell to the ground.

'As soon as we recovered a little from that awe and amazement at the presence of his majesty, we broke out with one voice, "We praise thee, O God, we acknowledge thee to be the Lord."

'This Pentecostal new year's day confirmed that the awakening had come and launched the campaign of extensive evangelisation which sprang from it.'[12]

The countdown begins

Considering what God did in Britain two centuries ago is both encouraging and highly instructive in helping us to understand the present time (see Romans 13:11).

God has preserved a faithful remnant of his people. Bands of men and women whose hearts God has touched are to be found in various parts of the church of Christ.

Intercessory prayer groups are springing up – and, for some, intercession is the burden of their lives. New pioneering and innovative efforts are being seen, particularly in the newer churches. Some of God's leaders have already begun to reach out to each other.

For sure, there needs to come a greater awareness of personal holiness. There still needs to be a more obvious return of the authoritative biblical preaching of the eighteenth century evangelists.

But the signs are clear: the countdown has begun to another great outpouring of the Holy Spirit. The best is yet to be!

NOTES

1. *Christian Leaders of the Eighteenth Century*, by J.C. Ryle, Banner of Truth, 1978

2. *The Inextinguishable Blaze,* by A. Skevington Wood, Paternoster Press, 1960

3. *Great Revivals,* by Colin Whittaker, Marshall Pickering, 1984

4. *The History of Christianity,* Lion Publishing, 1977

5. *Revival – Can we make it happen?,* by Dr Martyn Lloyd-Jones, Marshall Pickering, 1986

6. Op. cit.

7. *George Whitefield,* by Arnold Dallimore, Banner of Truth, 1980

8. Ibid.

9. *Great Revivals,* op. cit.

10. Op. cit.

11. Quoted in *New Wineskins,* by Howard Snyder, Marshall Pickering, 1977

12. Op. cit.

Revival: What happens?

Alan Scotland

When revival comes, certain features are clearly evident

Revival is a visitation of God.

In the church's history there have been many remarkable occasions when God has visited his church. Some have been more localised than others, but each visitation has borne similar hallmarks to the early outpourings of the Spirit on the church at and after Pentecost.

We will highlight some of the hallmarks of revival from the Acts accounts (references are to Acts unless otherwise stated) and draw parallels from revivals since that time.

Power and glory in the church

The early church grew up with a strong sense of the nearness of God and the overwhelming power of the Spirit. Hardly a day seemed to pass without eventful encounters with God, as he moved on individuals (3:1-10; 8:26-39; 9:1-30), households (10:1-48) and whole communities (2:41; 5:27-28; 8:14).

These were powerful times of divine visitation. God by his Spirit swept into the kingdom huge numbers of converts, beginning with the three thousand at Pentecost (2:41). Each revival since has seen similar large-scale conversion. It is estimated that John Wesley, between 1739 and his death in 1791, saw an ingathering of some seventy-two thousand in Britain and some fifty-seven thousand in America.[1]

During the Great Awakening in the USA (1857-58) it was estimated that, in the northern parts alone, some fifty thousand converts per week came to the Lord for up to eight successive weeks.[2]

The effect of the 1904 Welsh Revival was far-reaching, well beyond the Principality itself. Those converted in Wales totalled over eighty-three thousand, and several hundred converts were reported within a few days in the north of England.[3] Over a period of two years, it was estimated that this revival affected almost five million people.[4]

Sovereign work of the Spirit

The operations of God's Spirit in revival are sovereign. Their scope and impact could not have been planned or organised by people – even though people have always been involved in preparation by prayer and obedience. God breaks in on his church suddenly, announcing his arrival in displays of power and judgment, and in acts of mercy.

'The wind blows wherever it pleases,' said Jesus, adding, 'So it is with everyone born of the Spirit' (John 3:8). That same Spirit came at Pentecost 'like the blowing of a violent wind . . . from heaven and filled the whole house where they were sitting' (Acts 2:2).

That is revival. Duncan Campbell described it as 'a going of God among his people and awareness of God laying hold of the community'.

Eager expectation

A great outpouring of the Spirit is often preceded by a sense of eager expectation.

Christ himself led the early apostles to expect a divine visitation. Had not God promised to pour water on him who was thirsty? His Father, he told them, 'will give you another Counsellor to be with you for ever — the Spirit of truth' (John 14:15-17). 'When he comes,' he added, 'he will convict the world of guilt in regard to sin and righteousness and judgment' (John 16:7-8).

Those days before Pentecost must have been shaped by this expectation. By meeting together regularly, calling upon God and encouraging one another with this hope they did more than just talk about the Holy Spirit: they made room for him to come. They took hold of the promise and appealed to God for its fulfilment — with dynamic effect.

When it happened — and whenever it has happened since — the experience has been no mere shower of blessing but a downpour. 'Exalted to the right hand of God,' said Peter of Jesus, 'he has received from the Father the promised Holy Spirit and has *poured out* what you now see and hear' (2:33).

Church profile heightened

When God turns up, there is no hiding the fact. D.N. Phillips is quoted as saying of the 1904 revival in Wales: 'The revival is the topic in all spheres and among all sections of the society, strong people are overwhelmed by reading the newspaper reports of it.'

The presence of God in such a measure has a powerful impact on the awareness of the community at large and brings the church into greater visibility. Indeed, visitations of God have always begun with the church — that is part of the divine strategy.

In revival the church becomes gripped by the reality of God. Its members are taken beyond merely celebrating the fact that God has turned up; they experience a powerful equipping

for the task which God himself has begun among them –
the task of preaching the gospel of the kingdom and extending
the rule of Christ.

Vision and prophecy

At such times God will often use visions to convey his strategy
for the spread of the gospel, like the one given to Peter in
Acts 10:9-22.

Such visions are no flowery poetry. They are made of the
stuff of reality, touching real life. Thus, while Peter pondered
the meaning of his vision, the men sent by Cornelius, having
located Simon's house, stopped at the gate. The Spirit said
to him, 'Simon, three men are looking for you.' The result:
people got radically saved, filled with the Spirit and baptised
in water.

True revival, and the visions that go with it, are more than
the revealing of God's heart. They involve the doing of God's
will. For God himself is no mere visionary. He is a doer, and
those caught up in a divine visitation are compelled into
action. Peter *acted* on his vision. 'The Spirit told me to have
no hesitation about going with them,' he reported later
(11:12).

Prophecy, too, is practical and directive at such times. God
will communicate through prophecy places to visit and people
to see, people whom the Holy Spirit has prepared beforehand.
Usually there is a hunger for God in these people – and the
results are outstanding (11:27; 13:2).

Miracles and powerful preaching

The miraculous happenings that take place (such as 5:19;
8:26; 12:7-10) are not just remedial, that is, putting right
physical problems and bringing about sudden healings. They
are divine interventions of God, sometimes involving angelic
appearances.

God is pursuing his work with vigour. So, when Philip and the Ethiopian eunuch came up out of the baptismal water, 'the Spirit of the Lord suddenly took Philip away, and the eunuch did not see him again, but went on his way rejoicing' (8:39).

The powerful preaching of Philip is mirrored in that of the preachers God has used in subsequent revivals. It was said of Whitefield, for example, that 'he preached like a lion. His sermons were life and fire; you must listen whether you like it or not. There was a holy violence about him which firmly took your attention by storm'.[5]

Sensitivity in the Word

When Peter explained to the crowd at Pentecost what God was doing among them, he showed powerful revelation in the understanding of Old Testament Scripture. His spelling out of what God was doing in the light of the Word produced great conviction of sin and turning to the faith.

Stephen, too, before and during his stoning, displayed a sensitivity to the Spirit and unusual wisdom in expounding the Word (6:8 – 7:60). And Philip clearly moved in the effective delivery of the Word, backed up with miracles, healings and the expulsion of demons (8:5-7).

Paul, also, was mighty in the Word, using it sensitively to silence his religious opponents (9:22). And great preachers in every revival since have known a similar anointing to preach the Word with power and effect.

Spontaneous response

Every visitation of God sees spontaneous responses to his presence. Sometimes people cry out or fall down under conviction. This reflects the spontaneity of God himself, who sometimes bursts in and interrupts the programme. This was the case when Peter had no sooner begun to speak than the

Holy Spirit came upon the people and brought his preaching
to a halt (11:15-18).

Duncan Campbell describes a more recent instance (during
the Lewis revival of 1948-52) this way:

'A wave of revival swept the village. I could only stand
in silence as wave after wave of divine power swept through
the house, and in a matter of minutes following this heaven-
sent visitation men and women were on their faces in distress
of soul. Some weeping in sorrow and distress, others, with
joy and love filling their hearts, falling upon their knees,
conscious only of the presence and power of God who had
come in revival blessing.'[6]

Pioneering spirit

It is common for revival to bring a pioneering spirit to the
church. God turns his people, with their tendency to become
inward-looking, into a dynamic, outgoing community that
invades every stratum of society.

Evangelism becomes not so much an organised event as
a compelling witness to what God is doing among them as
believers. On the street, in the marketplace, they reach lives
with the gospel and arouse great curiosity (2:5-13; 8:4, 40).

And if boldness begins to wane, effectual prayer quickly
restores it. The early believers prayed persuasively, God
responding by filling them again with the Holy Spirit and
physically shaking the place. A similar shaking of a house
through prayer is reported from the Lewis revival.[7]

Awe and conviction of sin

At such times the fear of God not only comes upon the church
but also spills over into the community at large. 'Everyone
was filled with awe' (2:43), and the church in Judea, Galilee
and Samaria continued to live 'in the fear of the Lord' (9:31).

In particular, men and women are gripped with the

conviction of sin (2:37; 16:29-30). The word 'awakening' is an apt word to use in this connection. As people's hearts are opened up they begin to see the greatness of their need and feel the awesomeness of God's presence.

This conviction – a characteristic of the Spirit's operation (John 16:8) — is often so great that it grips them physically and mentally with torment and physical trembling, as in the case of the Philippian jailer. 'Trembling grips the godless: "Who of us can dwell with the consuming fire? Who of us can dwell with everlasting burning?" ' (Isaiah 33:14. See also Daniel 10:10; Hosea 11:10).

Just as Moses, reflecting on his own close encounters with God and their physical effect on him, said, 'I am trembling with fear' (Hebrews 12:21), so the woman healed of her haemorrhage was physically gripped by the reality of what had happened to her (Mark 5:33).

Revival produces similar effects. James Robe, in his *Records of the Kilsyth and Cambuslang Revivals*, writes, 'I have two very strong men in my remembrance while I write this; they had been several hours under distress before I saw them.'

Finney was clear about such experiences of spiritual distress, but he also knew the key to release. 'Generally,' he writes, 'you will find that conviction of the Spirit is deep and pungent, but short if handled correctly. Protracted seasons of conviction are generally owing to defective instruction. Wherever clear and discriminating instructions are given to convicted sinners they will generally find release after a short time.'[8]

Changed relationships

No-one can remain the same once they have encountered God in such a way. Peter could vouch for this, having come through dealings with God over his attitude to the Gentiles. 'God has shown me,' he reported, 'that I should not call any

man impure or unclean. So when I was sent for, I came
without raising any objection' (10:28-29).

Such transformations in people's lives through contact with
the power of God are radical, astonishing the people who
knew them before (9:20-21; 4:13). Every revival has had
its examples.

Community reaction

There has never been a revival in the church which hasn't
had a dramatic effect upon the community at large.

Some of the reaction is hostile, for all religion that denies
the power of God is threatened when revival takes place. Fear
and jealousy are exposed in traditional circles. It was so with
the early church, and subsequent visitations of God have come
under serious attack from the religious institutions.

But overall, the effects are wonderfully positive. The crime
rate drops as people are born again in large numbers. Occult
practices suffer a severe blow at the hand of the kingdom's
unrelenting progress.

In Wales, the social impact of the revival became proverbial.
It was said that the pit ponies could no longer understand
the miners' instructions because of the absence of oaths and
curses. The most notable effect of that revival was the sharp
decline in drunkenness.[9]

May we be gripped by the truth that God will yet visit the
earth in a greater outpouring than any seen since Pentecost.
More than that, let us be expectant and make room for it
to happen.

It would be naive to believe that such a visitation would
be welcomed by all. But let the cry of each who loves him
be, 'O Lord, revive your work, and begin in me.'

NOTES

1. *The Radical Wesley: Patterns for Church Renewal,* by Howard A. Snyder,
   IVP

2 . *Revivals of Religion: The Welsh Revival of 1904,* by Charles G. Finney, Morgan Scott, 1913

3 . *Welsh Revival of 1904,* by Eifion Evans, Evangelical Press of Wales, 1974

4 . *In the Day of thy Power,* by Arthur Wallis, CLC, 1956

5 . *Christian Leaders of the Eighteenth Century,* by J.C. Ryle, Banner of Truth, 1978

6 . *The Lewis Awakening,* by Duncan Campbell, The Faith Mission, Edinburgh

7 . Ibid.

8 . Op. cit.

9 . Eifion Evans, op. cit.

Why revivals fade

Ivor Hopkins

*Every revival so far has come to an end. Is this inevitable?
Is the fading God's intention, or are there human factors
which could prevent it?*

'It was a blessed season, perhaps the most extensive in its
operation that we have ever known among us. But it has,
in great measure, passed away . . . Christians . . . keep
together, cherishing the memory of the time, blessing and
praying for its return.'[1]

Those who have experienced revival look back on those
days with profound yearning. It was the greatest thing that
ever happened to them, and until the tide returns they are
left like stranded mariners, waiting for the waves of blessing
to come again.

This sentiment is repeatedly echoed in the history of
revivals: 'You are brought into touch with the power of the
world to come, and something indefinable lives with you.
You can never be content with anything less than you have
seen; and you live to see it again.' This is the voice of a witness
of the Hebridean revival of 1949.

From the same move of the Spirit another adds, 'We still

feel we are a waiting community, waiting for the breath from heaven.'

Revivals seem to be brief outpourings of divine energy which awaken God's people to eternal realities. And through this awakened company God's purposes are powerfully advanced and accelerated in history. But until now revivals have, like the tide, always receded. God must have his good reasons for this, but what are some of the possible causes at the human level? Why do revivals fade?

Revival or religion?

They are often called 'revivals of religion'. Yet there is often little love lost between an incoming wave of divine blessing and the 'church' it comes to bless. The question we should ask is, 'Is religion a friend or foe of Holy Spirit outpourings?'

There is much evidence to suggest that religious routines of every kind, rituals, liturgies and niceties of 'religious' aesthetics are not given the time of day in times of spiritual awakening. Indeed, because all such religious machinery is man-made and not of divine origin, it becomes totally redundant when God's Spirit takes direct action.

Equally, the religious establishment is not noted for its enthusiastic zeal in either promoting or embracing an incoming wave of the Spirit.

'The revival is an epidemic, an extravagant manifestation of a spirit of religious fervour, or perhaps furore, which is rapidly becoming fanaticism' is the shrill voice of the high church concerning a remarkable move of God which began with a prayer meeting in New York, then swept through the USA and the UK in 1858-9.[2]

We catch a glimpse of the latent tension between a revivalist and church leaders in the following report on Evan Roberts during the Welsh revival of 1904-5:

'A striking fact was the joyous and radiant happiness of the evangelist. It has been remarked that the very essence of Roberts' campaign was *mirth*. To the rank and file church ministers, this was the most incomprehensible quality. They had always regarded religion as something iron-bound, severe, even terrible. Evan Roberts smiled when he prayed, laughed when he preached.'[3]

There are always enemies of revival outside the people of God, but they cannot stop the flow of the Holy Spirit. Opposition from *within* the professing church and from the ranks of those who see themselves as protecting the interests of 'true religion', however, can and do impede the advance of God's power.

Here is a searching warning from Ralph Mahoney, founder of the World Missionary Plan: 'God gives religious people a good excuse to stumble at what he is doing. You can miss God's visitation because of your preconceptions. I know people who have prayed for years that God would send a revival and, when it came, they rejected it.'

One is reminded of Stephen's words before the Sanhedrin: 'You stiff-necked people, with uncircumcised hearts and ears! You are just like your fathers: You always resist the Holy Spirit' (Acts 7:51).

In revival the conflict of the ages between God and his people comes into sharp focus, for opportunity is afforded to receive or resist God's Spirit.

Jonathan Edwards

Revival brings judgment to the household of God. Not only is sin exposed; unbiblical models of spiritual normality in the church and its structures are also uncovered.

When revival came to New England in 1740-42, Jonathan Edwards was one of its outstanding leaders. What took place in Northampton, USA, under his leadership was considered the best led of the revivals then sweeping the region. But, 'even in Northampton many things occurred which not only were deviations from decorum and good sense, but also prevailed to change . . . a *silent* and powerful work of divine grace into a scene of confusion and disorder'.[4]

Was there indeed confusion and disorder, or was the model of 'church' meetings one of sober, religious silence? If the latter, then the Spirit of God was expected to conform to those prevailing patterns which expressed the religious mind-set of that generation. He had to limit himself to their narrow conformity, whereas God's people must always enlarge their understanding to give full liberty to God.

When the Holy Spirit comes in power there can indeed be silence. Usually, however, such is the emotional intensity generated that the unrepentant feel as though they are in hell, and the revived jubilate as though they were already in heaven.

In the following year, 1743, one hundred and sixty ministers published an appreciation of the revival. Sadly, 'many of them regretted the extravagances and irregularities' which took place. What extravagances and irregularities? Here is a summary:

☐ Secret impulses were obeyed (promptings of the Holy Spirit?)

☐ Laymen invaded the ministerial office and, under the pretence of exhorting, had the audacity to preach

☐ Ministers failed to observe territorial boundaries and dared to preach in another's parochial patch

☐ Indiscreet young men rushed about preaching everywhere and at any time

The vested interests and territorial demarcations of these religious leaders seemed to them to represent religious normality. Not even God could be permitted to disturb their established order; it was sacred in their eyes and humanly, if not divinely, unalterable.

In reality, they had raised human barriers which hindered the advance of the awakening. Their norms allowed for no spontaneous promptings of the Spirit, nor preaching by those who, though not appointed by men, were anointed by God.

George Whitefield

George Whitefield was a man who burnt himself out for God. He too was greatly used in this outpouring of the Spirit in New England. Unfortunately he laboured in a religious strait-jacket.

He was accused of disorderly conduct: 'There can be no doubt that on Mr Whitefield these evils are to a considerable degree to be charged, as having first led the way in this career of irregularity and disorder.'

What specific accusations were brought against this man of God? Here is a summary of his 'sins':

☐ He discerned those who were unconverted

☐ He insisted that unconverted ministers be removed from their office

☐ He taught that, where this was not done, believers – individually and corporately – were to separate themselves from those who supported unconverted ministry

In a word, he believed that only the truly converted were real members of the church which is the body of Christ. Unconverted men could not be shepherds in the flock of God, nor could they be entrusted with the care of the sheep. This is a valid message still.

It was the Lord Jesus who said, 'Woe to you, teachers of the law and Pharisees, you hypocrites! You shut the kingdom of heaven in men's faces. You yourselves do not enter, nor will you let those enter who are trying to' (Matthew 23:13).

As a faithful doorkeeper in the house of God, Whitefield believed his work was ushering souls into the kingdom. It was his responsibility, as it is ours, to see that the entrance is unobstructed. Squatters, even ministerial ones, must not be allowed to block the way in, be they robed as priests, enthroned as prelates, or skilled with the eloquence of a Shakespearian actor. The ever-open door into God's kingdom is Christ, and no-one must be allowed to hinder access.

God's adjustments

God knows how to adjust his erring servants. The story is told of a missionary in the Congo revival in the 1950s who, on returning to his mission station, found it in the throes of a Pentecostal outpouring.

His staid evangelicalism was so appalled that he rushed out into the bush in horror. There God met with him, showing him a vision of blood flowing down over a rock. When it touched the boulder, the blood congealed. The Lord told his servant that this was a picture of his own heart, which was hindering the flow of his Spirit.

The missionary repented and returned to his African brethren who, worshipping God in tongues, ministered to the white man in Welsh, his native language.

Broken cisterns

'My people have committed two sins: They have forsaken me, the spring of living water, and have dug their own cisterns, broken cisterns that cannot hold water' (Jeremiah 2:13).

The first sin mentioned by the prophet is resolved when God's people turn back to him and drink of the water of life freely. But what of the second evil – broken cisterns? A cistern is a reservoir or tank for storing water. In spiritual terms, a cistern is a religious container which should hold the blessings of the Holy Spirit. But because it is a man-made, do-it-yourself cistern, it is useless as a container of divine life.

The same picture is in view when Jesus spoke of new and old wineskins. He said, 'Men [do not] pour new wine into old wineskins. If they do, the skins will burst, the wine will run out and the wineskins will be ruined. No, they pour new wine into new wineskins, and both are preserved' (Matthew 9:17).

The late Len Moules, former International Secretary of Worldwide Evangelisation Crusade (now WEC International), told of a missionary who witnessed revival in India in the 1930s. It crossed the continent as predictably as a railway timetable. Sad to say, when it had passed, it was as though it had never been. The existing cisterns could not hold the water.

Even today, denominational leaders believe their forms of worship, liturgies, orders of service and structures of church government are not in question. They believe revival will increase their numerical strength and leave their religious edifice intact.

But God requires our reservoirs to hold the water of life. Our wineskins must be capable of expanding with the fermentation of heaven's wine. Old wineskins are brittle; any sustained outpouring of divine energy will inevitably do irreparable damage to traditional church structures. The consequences of revival will be catastrophic for all broken cisterns and dried-out wineskins.

The true cistern for the life of God is not found in any religious system, be it ever so traditional or sanctified by age or state patronage.

Jesus said, 'Whoever believes in me . . . streams of living water will flow from within him' (John 7:38). He was telling his followers that Spirit-filled, believing people are the true wineskin.

A believing people in union with God become his working clothes: they see with his eyes, hear with his ears, speak with his voice and touch with his hands. This is revival. Immanuel, God with us by his Spirit, in person and in power!

Me with a quenchless thirst inspire,
A longing infinite desire,
And fill my craving heart.
Less than thyself, oh, do not give;
In might thyself within me live,
Come, all that thou hast and art.[5]

NOTES

1. R.C. Morgan, on the 1859 revival in Scotland, quoted in *The Fervent Prayer*, by J. Edwin Orr, Moody Press, Chicago, Illinois, 1974

2. *The Fervent Prayer*, op. cit.

3   *Revival: Principles to Change the World*, by Winkie Pratney, Whitaker House, 1983

4. *Works of Jonathan Edwards, Vol. 1*, Banner of Truth, 1974

5. Charles Wesley (1707-88)

The unacceptable face of revival

Roger Aubrey

*Nostalgia filters our memories. Revival has not always been
the time of unbroken glory we sometimes imagine*

If we are to believe all we read and hear about past revivals,
they seem to have been idyllic times. They were without
problem or opposition, with countless thousands entering the
kingdom of God. Accompanying this was great unity among
preachers and churches of all denominations.

While there is some truth in this, we must face the sad fact
that revivals have sometimes been marred by vehement
opposition and 'political' wrangling. During the Welsh
Revival of 1904-1905, for example, an incident occurred that
changed the whole course of the revival.

By the end of 1904, tremendous progress was being made
by Evan Roberts and his associates. It was estimated that
during the year some thirty-two thousand converts had been
made throughout Wales. Roberts himself was in excellent
spirits as the new year came. He was full of faith and in
excellent health, viewing the coming year with excitement,
for he had asked God for one hundred thousand souls.

What happened next effectively ended his part in the revival.

Letter to the press

On 31 January 1905, a letter appeared in the *Western Mail*, the national newspaper. It was a vitriolic attack on Evan Roberts by Peter Price, a Congregational minister from Dowlais, near Merthyr Tydfil.

Price made the claim that there had been two revivals going on, one true and the other false. The real revival was taking place in his own church at Dowlais. He accused the revival under Roberts of being nothing more than a blasphemy, an absolute sham. He also cast doubt on Roberts' intellectual capabilities, signing his letter 'Peter Price (B.A. Hons.), Mental and Moral Sciences Tripos, Cambridge (late of Queen's College, Cambridge)'.

This obviously jealous attack on Roberts' integrity provoked much debate and correspondence – which, incidentally, Roberts himself never entered into.

The revival hamstrung

While the support of the vast majority of people rested with Roberts, this outburst severely affected him, bringing about a sudden change in his behaviour. He was much more aware of opposition in his meetings than before, often naming people present who, he said, were hindering the Spirit of God.

This led to some unhappy incidents. In one he stopped people praying for a person whom he said was already damned.

Roberts' health began to suffer and he was advised to take a rest. The successful period of his ministry had come to an abrupt end within a few short weeks.

The rest of 1905 was taken up with visits to Liverpool and North Wales, with mixed results. By that autumn the influence of Evan Roberts was spent. He took part in occasional campaigns after these years, but was never really the same force again. He died in 1951.

Claiming credit

Even a man of the stature of F.B. Meyer was drawn into controversy over the revival. Right at its height, in late 1904, he unwisely attempted to take credit for it, claiming that his influence on Evan Roberts through the Keswick Movement was the foundation for what had become the revival.

This caused an uproar and provoked ill-feeling and hurt among the Welsh revivalists, distracting them from the matter in hand. This controversy went on long after the revival was over, and in some quarters is still a contentious issue today.

Certainly there were other major factors that caused the 1904 revival to go into decline, but there is no doubting that the hostility of Peter Price had a personal effect on Roberts from which he – and the revival – never really recovered. And the Keswick controversy left a bitter taste in the mouths of many, tarnishing the reputations of people and, more important, the testimony of God.

Lessons to learn

It is said that those who don't learn from the mistakes of history are condemned to repeat them. It is imperative that we learn the lessons of history if there is to be revival in our own day. Just as vital as prayer in sustaining revival blessing are the eradication of ungodly jealousy and political jostling, and the willing acknowledgement that the Holy Spirit can move outside our own sphere of activity.

The answer of one Welsh revivalist to F.B. Meyer displays the right attitude: 'Silence! Silence in the presence of the Lord! This is the Lord's doing, not yours directly or indirectly, and it is marvellous in our eyes.'

Does revival leave its mark?

David Matthew

Revivals must be of more than historical interest. The truths they recovered are for us to embrace today as part of God's progressive revelation through his Word

Hold your finger near enough to your eye and you can blot out the sun. How amazing – a piece of flesh and bone barely two centimetres wide hiding a burning sphere 1,392,000 kilometres across!

Most Christians do something like that with history. So engrossed do they become in their own work for God that they forget that others worked for God before them. They lose sight of the historical panorama of God's purpose. Great names from the past like Augustine, Luther, Wesley and Moody may ring a vague bell, but little more.

'So what?' some may ask. 'Does it really matter?'

Yes it does, because, as a rule, those who don't know where they have come from don't know where they are going either. It's all very well for Christians to condemn evolutionary humanism for its belief that the human race is adrift on a sea of chance, but they themselves are often just as lost when it comes to a sense of history.

History is a story, not of chance, but of purpose – *God's*

purpose. That is the Bible's clear teaching. There have been milestones in the outworking of that purpose, the most prominent being the coming of the Spirit at Pentecost. In that great event, God moved up a gear in the working out of his declared purpose: 'to bring all things in heaven and on earth together under one head, even Christ' (Ephesians 1:10).

Since then, history in general – and church history in particular – has been 'his story'. Let's stand back and try to see the shape of it.[1] In particular, we will aim to identify what each wave of revival has left behind.

Short-lived glory

The New Testament church began well, in life and vigour. Both paganism and die-hard Judaism felt the force of a people moving in the power of the Holy Spirit. Thousands got saved. Lives were transformed. Idol-makers went out of business.

Soon, however, the initial revival declined as Christians began to get set in their ways and ceased to listen to the Spirit. Whenever the Holy Spirit is quenched, something has to take his place if church life is to go on. Form began to replace spontaneity. Set orders of service, liturgies, episcopal posts, the erection of altars and such like came into being. The cold hand of ritualism soon gripped the body of Christ by the neck.

In spite of some leaders of outstanding scholarship and godliness who thrashed out the biblical doctrines of the Godhead, the church went rapidly downhill for the first six hundred years. No-one pretends that the New Testament church from which it descended had been perfect. Far from it! But it had enjoyed a life and spontaneity which quickly became a thing of the past.

During the Middle Ages the institutional church settled at an all-time low. Megalithic, dead Catholicism ruled men's lives. Sure, there were sparks of life during this period – often in the monasteries. Here and there an attempt was made to break out in reform. But, always, the sheer weight of the ecclesiastical system squashed the life out of it.

Turn of the tide

Not until the sixteenth century did things change drastically.

The Reformation, under spiritual giants like Luther and Calvin, saw an unprecedented breakout of spiritual life. In spite of the fact that it all got mixed up with politics, thousands were born again, with radical effect for good in society as a whole.

From that time on, a clear *pattern of revival and decline* became evident. A wave of revival would sweep up the beach, bringing with it long-neglected but now rediscovered biblical truths. In the case of the Reformation they were justification by faith (as opposed to works), the priesthood of all believers (as opposed to that of the clergy only) and the sufficiency of Scripture (as opposed to tradition).

In its rush of spiritual life the revival wave would, for a while at least, force aside the debris of traditional religious forms – after all, who needs forms when God himself is on the move? But then, because of the unwillingness of some Christians to embrace the new revelation, or because the vigour of the Holy Spirit's moving offended their religious formality, the wave would lose its force. Gradually it would recede and lose itself in the sea again.

But always there was something left behind on the beach of history – some gem of recovered truth for subsequent generations to enjoy.

What God meant for the embracing and enjoyment of all his people, however, was rarely received by them all. Refusal on the part of many forced those who did receive it to form a new denomination around the freshly-discovered truth. The revival that, in its early rush, promised unity, instead left behind greater fragmentation.

There is one more element in the cycle of revival and

decline, and it is the saddest of all: just as a receding wave
hinders the advance up the beach of the next wave, the new
denomination would join the older ones in not only resisting
but actively opposing whatever truth the Spirit chose to
highlight next. Thus Lutheranism opposed the further
insights of the Anabaptists, who recovered the truths of
believers' baptism by immersion and the need for separation
of church and state.

This is the tragedy of church history. God highlights truth
in order that all his people should embrace it. Hardhearted
and tradition-bound to the last, a majority have always resisted
it and, in so doing, have marginalised those with arms open
to receive it.

More waves up the beach

This pattern, begun in the sixteenth century, became well
established during the seventeenth and eighteenth. Revivals
appeared one after another, leaving behind them new gems
of biblical truth – and new denominations.

The early Baptists and other Independents recovered the
truth of the 'gathered church' – defining the church as born-
again people rather than as the mix of saved and unsaved of
cultural Christianity. They also stressed the autonomy of the
local church.

The church in the house, pioneered in the German revivals
under Philip Spener, found broader expression in Britain in
Wesley's class meetings. The Church of England, too hide-
bound to cope with the Evangelical Revival and a man who
cocked a snook at parish boundaries, stood by in alarm as
Methodism came into being.

John Fox, meanwhile, had witnessed a wave of revival
issuing in the Society of Friends, or Quakers. Their great
'truth'? The ability and right of each person to know within
himself the personal prompting of the Holy Spirit – a much-
needed antidote to rampant sacerdotalism and form-bound
religion.

The nineteenth century

'The Lord has more truth yet to break forth out of his holy Word,' John Robinson had declared to the Pilgrims in 1620, as they set sail for the New World to escape state interference in their faith. The passing years proved him right, and the nineteenth century was no exception, with yet more waves of revival coming up the beach, more long-lost truths recovered and more denominations formed.

The Second Evangelical Awakening flourished in the USA under evangelists Charles Finney and, later, Dwight L. Moody. A million Americans came to Christ in 1857-58 alone – the time when Moody himself became a believer and began his ministry. The blessing spilled over to Britain as he made many trips across the Atlantic.

Brethrenism came into being as a reaction to liturgical Christianity and the dominance of the clergy. In a desire to recapture New Testament simplicity, its adherents gave Christ the central place and allowed the Holy Spirit to direct their gatherings. Clergy/laity differences were laid aside. They divested the communion of its traditional ritual and met simply as 'brethren' to break bread in remembrance of Jesus.

Then the Salvation Army trumpeted its way on to the scene in a frontal attack on the devil's social strongholds, mirroring in Britain the great worldwide missionary endeavour which is the hallmark of the nineteenth century.

Each of these great movements represented a degree of revival. And, true to form, they left behind new denominations intent on holding fast the recovered truths. Among these truths were the social dimension of the gospel, the essential oneness of the body of Christ, the desirability of homegrown leadership and the need for world evangelism.

Closer to home

The outstanding revival of the present century must be the Pentecostal revival of 1906, born out of the earlier Welsh revival. Here, a vital experience of baptism in the Holy Spirit and his supernatural manifestations burst on the scene. Suddenly, First Corinthians began to make sense again.

Once more, the previous wave opposed this latest one. For all their beginnings in a move of the Spirit, the Brethren and the Salvation Army – not to mention the remnants of the older 'respectable' denominations – stood against the Pentecostal phenomenon. New denominations were thus formed. The Elim Alliance, the Assemblies of God and the Apostolic Church were added to the list, guarding the biblical treasure they had recovered.

More recently, the Pentecostal dimension has touched those in other denominations, too, in the charismatic movement which began in the sixties.

It has gone two ways. The 'renewal' stream is intent on the renewal of the existing denominations, while the 'restoration' stream longs for their demise and the emergence of the one church of Jesus Christ from among them all. Present-day apostles and prophets, they believe, will be a major factor in bringing it about.

In the meantime, revival runs apace in the third world. Africa, Latin America and the East have seen millions come to Christ. The nineteenth-century flow of missionaries from Britain and America to the world beyond is now being reversed.

One lesson to be learnt from this is that local churches can be big. Paul Yonggi Cho's church in South Korea is ample testimony. It also stands as a condemnation of the small-mindedness of many western Christians.

More waves to come?

This, then, is where we come from. Our history is a saga of divine patience. God has been working out his plan in spite of human weakness and selfishness. The question now is, what further truths remain to be recovered? What light is yet to break forth from God's holy Word?

Many believe the important emerging focus is Christian unity. As we have seen, revival has tended to unify God's people – but only for a while. The denominational barriers have not been fully dismantled during the rush of the Spirit. Always, Christians have put a 'Reserved' notice on some of their practices, refusing to let the Holy Spirit and the Word touch them.

And so the wave has lost its power. As the revival has faded the old systems have reasserted themselves and things have reverted to a substandard normal.

Happily, we need not continue this way. Scripture is still the objective standard against which we must measure our condition. It offers, not a legalistic blueprint, but clear, broad principles for both individual and church life. The revival movements of church history have highlighted those principles clearly enough. If we were all to reorder our personal and church life in the light of them, ditching the dead wood of non-biblical tradition, unity would emerge overnight.

At present, it seems, vested interest and blinkered thinking prevent that happening. So we pray for yet another revival. When it comes, God will offer us another chance to let the Spirit's wind blow away our accumulated rubbish. If we seize it, his purpose will take a great leap forward. If not, we condemn another generation to die in the wilderness.

It will not do to say that God will work out his purpose in his own way and his own good time. Scripture shows that God chooses to work through his people. Will his people be willing in the day of his power?

Better still, are we willing now?

NOTES

1. A fuller treatment of this theme is to be found in David Matthew's book, *Church Adrift*, Marshall Pickering, 1985, now distributed by Harvestime

The charismatic renewal: Is it revival?

Arthur Wallis

The charismatic movement is the most dramatic Christian development this century. What is its relationship to revival?

The charismatic renewal in the mid-sixties began with individual believers seeking the Father for his promised gift of the Holy Spirit.

Multiplied thousands all over the world have experienced the baptism in the Holy Spirit, with far-reaching results. They have received power through the oncoming of the Holy Spirit, spoken in new tongues, been set free from fears and inhibitions and have come into a new dimension of praise, prayer and worship.

Chapters 12 and 14 of 1 Corinthians, at one time incomprehensible, have now become clear and plain. And this for the simple reason that the wonderful gifts of the Father – tongues, interpretation, prophecy and such like – have been *experienced*, instead of being relegated to a museum of New Testament curiosities.

It is only a Spirit-baptised church that will bring in the kingdom of God. There is no bypassing the experience of renewal. What exciting days these are! But to look at the situation realistically, we are obliged to acknowledge ruefully that, by present standards, it is going to take thousands of years to see the kingdom triumph across the face of the earth.

But hold on. There is a weapon in God's armoury that he is still holding in reserve. It is *revival* – the divine break-in.

Few words in our spiritual vocabulary mean so many different things to so many different people. On the American continent 'revival' usually describes a series of evangelistic meetings: 'We plan to have a revival in our church next month.'

Others equate it with a personal renewal as individuals are sanctified, quickened or filled with the Holy Spirit.

Many think and speak of the charismatic renewal – the renewal *movement* – as revival. It was the seeking of God for revival, even before the charismatic movement broke out, that led many of us into a renewal experience. But even as we came into some experience of these things we knew that revival had not yet come.

Anyone who has read widely of the true revivals of the past will have no hesitation in affirming that we have not yet seen it in our generation, at least not in Britain. We have certainly seen valuable movements of the Holy Spirit that have had some of the ingredients of revival, but there have been significant missing elements.

There is a *visitation of God* in revival that is more powerful than anything we have ever experienced. When it first came, at Pentecost, it took the city of Jerusalem by storm. Three thousand were saved on the spot. Then we read, 'And fear came upon every soul' (Acts 2:43 KJV). Imagine that great metropolis, the centre of world Jewry, caught in the grip of God!

This feature has not been characteristic of the charismatic renewal, but it *is* characteristic of revival. Let us prepare ourselves for something grander than we have yet experienced. We shall see salvation without sermons, healing without imposition of hands and deliverance without a commanding word. The whole of society will know about it!

The crowning blessing of a true visitation of the Holy Spirit is a *mighty harvest for the kingdom of God.* But it is more than large numbers of converts. This can happen and does happen without revival. It is the *manner* in which they are converted. It is the depth of conviction of sin, the travail with which they come and are born into the kingdom. That is what catches the headlines.

The charismatic renewal has now been around for years. Yet many in our churches, not to mention the vast majority of our citizens, know nothing about it. They have not been touched by it. It is clear that the *community impact* has been minimal.

In true revivals, community impact is a major feature. People do not have to read the *Gospel Gazette* in order to discover that God is among his people. There are signs and wonders that fill men and women with awe. The message of the kingdom becomes the major talking-point in the pubs and the clubs. There may be debating and discussing, mocking and scoffing, but indifference is no longer possible.

When the great harvest begins to be gathered in, when people can neither deny nor explain what is happening, when indifference to the gospel is no longer possible, when sin hides its head in shame – then we will know that revival has truly come.

Reporting revival

David Lazell

Illustrations from the Welsh Revival of how the media handle a spiritual phenomenon

Exaggeration, misreporting and arousal of the emotions are all features of popular tabloid newspapers today, and Christian influence in the mass media is at a low ebb.

What is likely to happen when revival comes again? Will the new satellite TV channels find themselves reporting a new upsurge of national spirituality? Will the press and other media be interested, sympathetic, or will they merely indulge in sensationalism?

Generally speaking, Christians have reason to doubt even the reporting of lesser phenomena than revival.

One local newspaper homed in on the controversy provoked by the charismatic developments in an Anglican church. Though the minister was a well-respected man, the headline read, 'Vicar brings new cult to town'. I wrote to the editor, referring to Acts 2 and parallel developments in many other churches, but my note was ignored.

At Ephesus Paul found materialism to be the great opponent of revival. Nothing has changed. In the present materialistic

climate, a preacher calling for repentance in the biblical
fashion could be accused of stirring up trouble.

When I read in the narratives of the Welsh Revival that
miners stopped work to pray together and salesmen
abandoned their calls to go to church for afternoon meetings,
I can almost hear some present-day political leaders com-
plaining that such behaviour does not help productivity and
the beating of inflation.

Would Christians be ready to risk unpopularity in rebuking
the nation if, as may well be the case, revival were to come
at a time of great economic distress?

Slow reactions

While misunderstanding by the secular press is perhaps
understandable, Christian papers should know better. But
even they have often been slow to recognise the real issues.
In November 1904, Evan Roberts wrote a letter to Hartley
Aspden, editor of *The Sunday Companion*, adding a significant
comment: 'We are on the eve of a great and grand revival,
the greatest Wales has ever seen. Do not think the writer is
a madman.'[1]

Mr Aspden was responsible not only for that one paper
but for a number of Christian titles published by the
Harmsworth publishing house. He was thus in a position to
give wide coverage to the events beginning in Wales. Yet
though he responded courteously to Evan Roberts, he did
not take up the story until other sources confirmed that a
revival was indeed in hand.

He later explained to D.M. Phillips, Evan Roberts'
biographer, that having heard neither of Loughor (birthplace
of the revival, in south-west Wales) nor of Roberts himself,
he had concluded that the letter was just 'one of those strange
epistles' which reach editorial offices in every generation.
When, later, he was to hear about the revival, he was also

to learn that its leader was the 'man whose strange letter I had received'.

W.T. Stead – a sympathetic writer

Ironically, it fell to a somewhat unorthodox writer and man of religion, W.T. Stead, to bring enthusiastic coverage of the revival to a national readership. This he did through the pages of *The Review of Reviews*, which he edited, and the 'Revival Pamphlets' published under the magazine's imprint from its offices just off Fleet Street, London.

Stead believed that the affairs of religion deserved prominence in the press, and had shown this in his reports on the plight of teenage girls in London. Helped by Bramwell Booth and the Salvation Army, he had shown that it was entirely possible to purchase a teenage girl in the city.

His article, 'The Maiden Tribute of Modern Babylon', in the *Pall Mall Gazette*, caused outrage among those who saw him as attacking the great British Empire, and hope among genuine reformers who had long despaired of getting action from government on the age of consent.

Stead's reporting of the Welsh revival was influential and gave credibility to the cause, though it inevitably aroused controversy, even among church members. His 'Revival Pamphlets' were quite substantial affairs, the first being published at the very beginning of the revival. Especially valuable was the third, which looked back at the work of Gypsy Smith and the inter-church missions of the National Federation of Evangelical Free Churches (NCEFC).

The concern of the churches about a population drifting away from Christian belief went back decades and had prompted the missions of the first years of this century. A former editor of *The Western Mail* – the Cardiff morning newspaper which covered much of the 1904-5 revival – assured me that the missions conducted in Wales by Gypsy Smith prior to the work of Evan Roberts had prepared the way. To put it simply, Evan Roberts did not come 'from nowhere' but was himself the fruit of much prayer and labour.

W.T. Stead also recognised that the events in Wales were not exclusively Welsh in their impact, but signalled changes elsewhere. We tend to forget other notable preachers of that period such as Albert Shakesby, the converted athlete, who did so much good in Primitive Methodism and who was healed from injuries at Mow Cop.[2]

Rationalist opposition

Stead took up cudgels against all manner of people who showed disbelief or opposition to the effects and causes of revival. In the third 'Revival Pamphlet', for example, he tackled an article published in the *Literary Guide and Rationalist Review*, in which a certain F.J. Gould suggested that the conversions were transient.

The question, 'Do conversions last?' is of perennial relevance, and Mr Gould could refer to his own 'conversion' as a boy of thirteen, some thirty years earlier, the effects of which had totally faded. His reaction to the revival events now in progress was, he suggested, almost that 'of a converted cannibal, who looks on with mingled interest and aloofness at his still barbaric countrymen'. His case serves to remind us that many who begin well in revival can be lost through lack of nurture and discipleship.

Stead, perhaps uniquely among journalists of that time, could discuss these issues in psychological and social, as well as biblical, terms. It was easy, in English drawing-rooms or even in distant church conferences, to regard the events in Wales as merely cultural in expression – 'a form of native religion', or even the natural enthusiasm of a young man eager to change the world overnight. We might be surprised to see just how much the superior comments of those years parallel our own.

A broader perspective

In Stead's view, Evan Roberts was just one part of the stream of renewal of the nation, not its prime source, and it is significant that he referred often to the self-sacrifice of the Welsh people. Revival comes, he seemed to say, to people who are serious about religion.

'Nothing is more certain,' he wrote, 'than that, if there had been no more prayer in proportion to the population in Wales than in London, there would have been no revival. It was the incessant, persistent, won't-be-denied kind of praying that lit the flame in South Wales.'

He was writing at a time when the evangelistic campaigns in London under Americans R.A. Torrey and C.F. Alexander were facing difficulties – though he viewed them as part of the great revival movement.

'If the proprietors of the Albert Hall,' he wrote, 'would hand it over rent free to the Torrey-Alexander mission, as the proprietors of the Welsh chapels hand them over rent free to Evan Roberts, much expense would be saved.'

He seemed to be arguing that, because revival would do such great good to the nation, everyone should help as far as possible in order to achieve the end result. That, one imagines, would hardly go down well in the cash-nexus society of our own day.

Evan Roberts defended

The presence of Christian employees in the secular press helped to ensure favourable coverage on the whole, and the extent of this can be seen by the references in recent studies on the Welsh Revival.

Naturally, not all writers view it with equal sympathy. Evan Roberts' work has been recently recalled by Tom Davies, whose novel, *One Winter of the Holy Spirit*, is set against the Wales of the revival period. There, Evan's work is shown as culminating in the collapse of 1906 and – as far as the book is concerned – the end of the revival itself.

However, Dr J. Edwin Orr, in the years prior to his death, defended the good name of Evan Roberts following the publication of some critical articles in, of all papers, that same *Western Mail* which had reported the revival so sympathetically in its day.

In March 1985, Dr Orr wrote to me: 'It is true that Evan Roberts suffered physical breakdown in 1907. He was still an invalid when I had cordial fellowship with him from 1934 onwards, but his mind was clear. In 1934 I toured every county in Wales and found converts of the revival very active.

'This is confirmed in Iain Murray's biography of Dr Martyn Lloyd-Jones (p278), where, quoting a Canadian journalist in the mid-1930s, he writes: "How much is left today of the result of the great Evan Roberts revival?"

' "I affirm," said Lloyd-Jones, "that of the best Christian leaders we have in Wales today, a vast proportion are products of that Welsh revival."

'From church growth statistics, I find that 82.5 per cent of the converts were persevering in 1909. Roy Pointer's book on church growth shows sustained Baptist membership in west Glamorgan for more than a generation.'

Inevitably, the events of the Welsh Revival focus upon that single young man, and we may well forget the tremendous burden placed upon the shoulders of one whose training was very limited. It is to his credit that he could be recalled with such affection decades after the event. And Dr Orr took time from a busy schedule to conduct meetings to defend Roberts' good name, seventy years after Roberts launched into that great work.

But in the end, revival is about far more than the work of a single man. And it is to a very large degree beyond mere intellectual debate or understanding.[3]

The lessons for our time are obvious. Revival is not

welcomed by some entrenched forces in society, and even in religious structures. The great unsettling ahead will be a shaking of the nation – but with immense good beyond it, and a better ordering of human priorities. For the media it will be, in a sense, an early day of judgment.

NOTES

1. *Evan Roberts – The Great Welsh Revivalist and His Work,* by D.M. Phillips, Marshall Brothers, 1906

2. *From Street Arab to Evangelist – The life story of Albert Shakesby, a converted athlete, by himself,* Burtt Brothers, Hull, 1910

3. See *The King's Champions – Revival and Reaction, 1905-1935,* by B.P. Jones, published privately by the author from The Manse, Glascoed, Pontypool, Gwent. 1986 reprint of 1968 original

Part Two

Looking forward to coming revival

'The earth will be filled with the knowledge of the glory of the Lord, as the waters cover the sea'

Habakkuk 2:14

Clarifying our expectations

Bryn Jones

We often talk about coming revival, but what exactly do we envisage?

Suddenly it was different. The hush in the room was not the silence of people not knowing what to say but that of people unable to say anything. God's presence filled the place.

Only minutes before, there had been tiredness. It was past midnight but the room was filled with men and women praying that God would pour his Spirit upon his church. This was just one of many such prayer meetings held around that time. There was a sense of God's wanting to break in upon his people.

I held my breath. I could sense he was close – so very close. Even to breathe, I felt, would break the atmosphere of divine presence. Then someone cried, 'Oh God, oh God!' and people began to weep. I felt my body convulse with shaking as I dissolved in tears on the floor.

I don't know how many hours we lay there weeping. I wasn't conscious of any prayer other than the groans, sighs and travailing sounds around me. When finally we rose from that prayer meeting I looked at the bare pine floorboards and

saw how the tears had soaked into the wood, leaving them
stained.

Meetings like that went on for many months during 1955-57
in South Wales. Their intent: revival. But what do we mean
by that word? What did those travailing believers mean by it?

Religious romanticism

For me at that time revival meant a repeat of what had taken
place in 1904-05 in those same regions: chapels crowded with
people calling on God for mercy and grace; public houses
emptying as men surged into the kingdom of God; the air
resounding with God's praises; the valleys filled with singing.

It was a vivid picture of revival power painted on my mind
by men and women only too eager, in their latter years of
life, to share their memories of 'the great revival of 1904'.
Although praying with such people has left an indelible
stamp upon my soul, I realise in retrospect that the religious
romanticism of that picture of revival served to close my mind
to other vital issues intended by God's visitation.

Today, when thousands of God's people are being stirred
afresh to cry for revival, it is vital that we face up to some
fundamental questions if we are to see our prayers answered
and reap lasting benefit from the visitation when it comes.

Sharpening our focus

It is difficult to capture the meaning of revival in a single
statement. Phrases like 'divine visitation', 'spiritual awakening' and 'outpouring' spring readily to mind.

Certainly revival is greater in its impact than that of a
normal evangelistic campaign and very different from the all-
too-predictable 'Sunday services'. It is the visitation of God's
Spirit upon his people, bringing an exceptional awareness
of his presence in the church, and this accompanied by great
demonstrations of his power and life.

Times have changed since the revival in Wales at the opening of this century. Today people are intellectually more sophisticated, politically more aware. Science calls God into question as never before. Humanism and materialism dominate the lives of millions. In our largely secular society the Christian church is seen as a quaint leftover from the past and religion too compromised to be relevant to the needs of the masses.

Yet our prayer for revival must not be based on the state of our world and the desperate plight of humankind. Neither does God feel obliged to answer prayers based on religious nostalgia over empty chapels and church buildings being sold off as warehouses or turned into luxury apartments.

God has only one basis on which he will be entreated, and that is his own Word. To release faith for revival I must find the basis for my prayer in the promises of God. Here is where I find my grounds for confident petition in the courts of heaven.

A scriptural basis for revival?

The worldwide triumph of the church is implicit in the very first promise of a Redeemer given in Eden: 'I will put enmity between you [Satan] and the woman, and between your offspring and hers; he will crush your head, and you will strike his heel' (Genesis 3:15).

God further implied worldwide blessing when he promised Abraham, 'All peoples on earth will be blessed through you' (Genesis 12:3).

The promise surged on in his word to Moses that, though God be reduced to just this one man, he would still accomplish his purpose of filling the earth with his glory (Numbers 14:21-24).

It is there again in the covenant with David guaranteeing the eternal rule of his seed upon his throne, fulfilled in Jesus (Acts 2:29-31).

Isaiah spoke of it, stating that in the last days 'the mountain of the Lord's temple will be established as chief among the mountains' (Isaiah 2:2). The implication is that the church of Jesus Christ will have power and influence exceeding that of the nations around.

It is there in Joel's great prophecy that in the last days God would pour out his Spirit upon all flesh so that the sons and daughters of God would prophesy (Joel 2:28). This promise, Peter later explained, extended beyond the Pentecost generation to the conclusion of this present age, in which God is calling men to himself (see Acts 2:39).

And so we could go on through the prophets, quoting Ezekiel, Jeremiah, Zechariah, Malachi and others.

It is our knowledge of his will through his Word that gives us our basis of confidence in approaching God for revival. This is far more vital than knowing that Smith Wigglesworth, John G. Lake, D.L. Moody or any other great man of the past has prophesied such a visitation.

What can we expect to happen?

1. Revival will bring change

We dare not, with some misguided Christians, restrict these Old Testament prophecies to the nation of Israel or see them merely as forecasting the experience of Pentecost two thousand years ago.

The apostle Peter pointed the way forward. *'Repent,'* he said, 'and turn to God in order that seasons of *refreshing* might come to you, leading to the *restoration* of all things and Christ's *return'* (see Acts 3:18-26). The order is important: repentance and turning come before the repeated revivals or 'seasons of refreshing'.

Next comes restoration. In every revival God reveals truth which, when received and obeyed, will help achieve his objectives in the earth. Each such 'word' from God is meant to become the 'walk' of his people, climaxing with the restoration of all things, as he promised through the prophets.

To talk, as some do, of 'restorationist groups', 'restoration churches' or a 'restorationist movement' is to miss the point. It marks a failure to understand the purpose of God. This isn't a denominating badge some Christians wear. God is restoring his church; God is restoring his people; God is restoring our world; God is restoring 'all things' in heaven and on earth!

We must not think, then, that restoration is merely a modification of existing evangelical practice – or indeed, that it is confined to visible things at all, for restoration touches on the world beyond the veil as much as on the visible world.

God is restoring *all* things – and that's what revival is ultimately about. Revival means change. Revival embraces the return of God's people to his Word and ways. Revival is the Spirit refreshing the church with revelation. Revival is the bringing to completion of everything promised in the divine programme.

Revival and restoration are thus inseparable. Restoration is not taking the church backwards to its original condition, but forwards to God's original intention – not back to its cradle but on to its maturity. To separate revival from restoration is to make revival an end in itself – to make it 'revival*ism*'. And who could be satisfied with that?

No, revival, because it is linked with restoration, will demand change; indeed, it will be characterised by change. And all this is *in order that* Christ can return (see Acts 3:19-20). There will be a final season of refreshing – revival – that will bring forth the capstone to all truth and introduce the church to the fulness of all that the prophets foresaw. This will then be the signal in the heavens for the return of Christ.

2. Revival will bring judgment

Revival means judgment for the house of God. We have to face up to deep issues, such as the challenge of Christ's prayer for the unity of his body, 'that the world may believe' the Father sent him (John 17:21).

The impact of conviction that leads to conversion is tied to the demonstration of the unity of God's people.

Let us not deceive ourselves by insisting that this unity is an invisible union of God's children irrespective of doctrinal differences or denominational affiliation. The world cannot see spiritual things – they understand only the visible. They judge by outward appearance, and not only are the present divisions in Christendom abhorrent to God, they also negate our message to the world.

We are saying to the world around, 'Exchange your divisions for ours, exchange your secular competitiveness for our brand of religious competitiveness. Leave your socio-political quest and join our religio-political confusion instead.'

This isn't the gospel Jesus Christ preached. He came with the all-embracing love of God for mankind. It is time we faced up to it: evangelicalism with its deep rifts is as detestable to God as any other manifestation of human division. His judgment hangs over it. Revival demands that we change.

3. Revival will impact the world

Do we expect revival to touch only the religious world? God forbid!

Nowhere in Scripture is there the suggestion that God is interested only in affecting religious life. God comes to people. God comes to men and women everywhere. When God visits, nothing remains untouched by his presence.

Looking at the social, religious and political ferment of our times, we see the spread of Islamic fundamentalism throughout the Middle East becoming increasingly militant among Western nations – exemplified in the Salman Rushdie affair. We see unrest sweeping through Eastern Europe, where the rise of resurgent nationalism among the ethnic minorities of the Soviet Union is causing everyone to ponder what its future will be.

We are witnessing the collapse of the communist empire. From time to time, totalitarian regimes exert violent effort to retain their despotic rule. The massacre in Beijing's Tiananmen Square tore the reformist mask from China's totalitarian communist rulers. The old-guard hardliners showed themselves as fascists seeking to stifle the human cry for freedom. Yet God is still at work in China despite decades of totalitarianism.

We see Africa's notorious buckling under the burden of debt, famine, war and disease. Can some of its nations even survive this century?

Then again, what of the new role for Britain in the European Community and the changes this will bring to family life through increased mobility of the workforce? Does all this cause us to fear, or do we say, 'God, what a tremendous opportunity to display your glory'?

With revival, we can expect God to break in politically, to address the social issues of our hurting world. Revival will affect the ethics and moral attitudes of our time. There will be no part of human endeavour or interaction that will not be affected by the spiritual awakening.

This surely is the implication of Zechariah, who saw in such a visitation a time when the very pots and pans of the kitchens would have 'holy to the Lord' written on them and the bells around the necks of the horses would carry the same inscription (Zechariah 14:20). What he is saying is that the lines separating the spiritual and secular will disappear; everything will be a spiritual issue before the Lord.

Revival will mean that you are as much in touch with God in your kitchen or workshop as you are in a cathedral or chapel. Wherever we look in our world today, God is greater than the issues of our time, and we can rejoice that his visitation will affect all that we see.

4. Revival will address the cry for justice

The very foundation of God's throne is righteousness and

justice (Psalm 97:2), and any genuine spiritual awakening will address both those issues. God will bring about whatever changes are necessary for men and women to rise free from the bondage of their oppressors.

We dare not wait for revival before we address such issues. It is blatant hypocrisy, an evil thing, that large numbers of 'Christian' people in South Africa continue to support the apartheid system. It is time God's children realised that, if we want God present among us in power and glory, we have to 'prepare the way' of his coming by taking whatever action is necessary *now* to sweep away those acts and attitudes that cannot co-exist with his presence.

Religion has always managed to accommodate injustice if to act justly has threatened its hierarchy or power base. Reinhold Niebuhr wrote, 'There is no social evil, no form of injustice, whether of the feudal or the capitalist order, which has not been sanctified in some way or other by religious sentiment and thereby rendered more impervious to change.'

Let's face things squarely: you cannot be a follower of Christ and a supporter of apartheid, however updated, modified or reformed it appears.

You simply cannot be a disciple of Christ and a racist. You cannot be a child of the kingdom of God and a supporter of divisions between people. You cannot claim God as your Father and at the same time deny some members of the human family. There is no difference in Christ between black and white.

5. Revival will affect the environment

The visitation of God will restore man's sense of responsibility towards the environment.

In creating man, God not only bestowed dignity upon him by making him in his own image; he also gave him the inestimable privilege of ruling the earth on his behalf.

Man's first task was to make his environment beautiful and

productive. As a result of the fall, however, man not only experienced death within himself but also lost his sense of destiny with respect to the world about him. Man has become the destroyer, not the keeper, of his environment.

The welcome emergence of the Green Movement (New Age connections aside) and the emphasis on environmental issues by it and other groups remind us that man and his environment are mutually bound together.

Man's continuing failure in his responsibility to care for his world is leading to unimaginable catastrophe. Wholesale slaughter of the animal world, asset-stripping of mineral resources from the ground, destruction of the rain forests, pollution of our rivers and oceans – all reflect a shortsighted policy of greed that says man has no concern for his children's future.

Revival will not simply renew man's commitment to God and his fellow-man, but will renew his commitment to the environment. By restoring his sense of responsibility it will cause him to commit himself afresh to this aspect of the purpose for which God created him.

6. Revival will produce a radical church

A radical church is desperately needed, a church that will advance the kingdom in all the world.

The visitation of the Spirit at Pentecost empowered a hundred and twenty people to move out across the nations of the world, turning city after city upside down. Their only allegiance was to the lordship of Christ. They supported no other party, adopted no other name, embraced no other cause than that of Christ and his kingdom.

This surely will be the repeated consequence of the visitation of God to a final generation. A radical church will emerge, a people fired with his fire, loving what he loves, hating what he hates. They will overturn unrighteousness and establish righteousness, breaking the chains of injustice and liberating men and women justly. Anointed with God's

Spirit, they will confront their age with the power of his kingdom.

The lines of demarcation between the world and the church will be clearer than ever before. Her unity will challenge the divided world. Her faith will rule over the world's unbelief. The holiness and power of God's people will draw the bruised, soiled and broken to seek Christ.

Then we will see the prophetic word fulfilled. The mountains will flow down at his presence, the desert will blossom like a rose. The trees will clap their hands, the mountains and hills will skip around. Those who were thirsty will find their thirst assuaged. Those who have longed for his salvation will see the salvation of the Lord their God.

Revival will meet every aspiration of God's people and move them forward in God's restoring purpose. Revival will touch the issues of righteousness and justice in the realm of money, ethnic relationships, cultural differences, personal attitudes and denominationalism. God will impact our world with his coming, righting the wrongs and freeing the bound.

Communism is already showing signs of crumbling. Materialism, secularism and humanism will follow, along with Islam, Hinduism, Buddhism and other Christless religions. Christ, and Christ alone, will be triumphant. And this, says Paul, is God's ultimate intention, that in all things Christ will have the supremacy (Colossians 1:18).

' "Shout and be glad, O Daughter of Zion. For I am coming, and I will live among you," declares the Lord. "Many nations will be joined with the Lord in that day and will become my people. I will live among you and you will know that the Lord Almighty has sent me to you. The Lord will inherit Judah as his portion in the holy land and will again choose Jerusalem. Be still before the Lord, all mankind, because he has roused himself from his holy dwelling" ' (Zechariah 2:10-13).

This is the ultimate revival.

The Old Testament basis for revival hope

Hugh Thompson

*Even before Christ's first coming, the prophets used graphic
images to foretell the great end-time revival*

Our hopes of worldwide revival must find their foundation
in the Word of God. My purpose here is twofold. First, to
draw out some of the Old Testament promises to that effect.
And second, to see whether the New Testament's treatment
of those promises indicates a fulfilment before our Lord Jesus
returns (as distinct from after, as some prophetic schemes
teach).[1]

Let us, then, highlight some major revival themes.

1. Seasonal rain – for a healthy harvest

'Repent,' Peter exhorted, 'and turn to God, so that . . . times
of refreshing may come from the Lord, and that he may send
the Christ . . . He must remain in heaven until the time
comes for God to restore everything, as he promised long
ago through his holy prophets' (Acts 3:19-21).

Peter here reckons that the Old Testament prophets
expected seasons of refreshing to precede Messiah's return

from heaven. They taught that the spiritual pattern of church history would resemble the weather pattern of the Old Testament agricultural year.

'The *former* [*autumn*] *rain* falls in the latter part of October or the first part of November usually. It is this rain that is the signal for the farmer to begin his ploughing and plant his seed. The Bible also speaks of the *latter* [*spring*] *rain*, which ordinarily falls in March and April, and it is this rain that is of so much value in maturing the barley and wheat crops.'[2] Between the two come intermittent winter showers.

God had covenanted, 'I will send rain on your land *in its season*, both autumn and spring rains, so that you may gather in your grain, new wine and oil' (Deuteronomy 11:11-14).

Spiritually speaking, then, the *autumn* rain of the Spirit, which enabled the seed of the kingdom to germinate, fell from Pentecost throughout the lifetime of the original apostles. During the centuries since then, churches here and there have experienced occasional winter showers – 'times of refreshing'. But we still await the *spring* rains, another significant outpouring of the Spirit which will prepare us for 'the harvest [which] is the end of the age' (Matthew 13:39).

Zechariah urges us to 'ask the Lord for rain in the springtime' because 'he gives showers of rain to men' (Zechariah 10:1). James implies that we ought to intercede for both autumn and spring rains before the Lord's coming (James 5:7-9, 17-18). This will mean an acceleration in the spiritual rain cycle so that 'the reaper will be overtaken by the ploughman and the planter by the one treading grapes' (Amos 9:11-15, which will be fulfilled during this age, according to Acts 15:12-18).

2. Sudden glory – God is at home, shaking everything 'out there'

After recounting how God shook the earth at the *birth* of

Judaism when he gave the law to Moses on Mount Sinai, the writer to the Hebrews mentions God's Old Testament promise that 'once more I will shake not only the earth but also the heavens' (Hebrews 12:25-29).

He foresaw the partial fulfilment of that shaking in the *burial* of Judaism when the Roman legions would destroy the Jerusalem temple in AD 70 and cause Levitical offerings to cease for ever.

The promise of shaking, quoted in Hebrews, comes from Haggai chapter two. The prophet originally gave the promise to the remnant of the Jews who had just begun to rebuild Solomon's temple after the exile in Babylon. The rebuilding was in preparation for the Messiah – 'the desired of all nations' (v7, compare 1 Samuel 9:20) – to visit it and work miracles of healing in its courtyards. As a result of that visitation 'the glory of this present house,' said Haggai, would exceed 'the glory of the former house' (2:9).

In the course of time this came to pass. But wonderful as it was, that could not be the end of the story since Hebrews 12, written after Christ's coming, predicted that the biggest shaking was still future. Clearly, therefore, the filling of God's house with the greatest glory was to occur after the demolition of the material temple. It would be the filling of a *spiritual* temple, namely, the church of Jesus Christ (1 Corinthians 3:16; 2 Corinthians 6:16; 1 Peter 2:5).

On this basis, Pentecost was the 'former glory' of God's spiritual temple (Haggai 2:3). Note that it was a *sudden* filling of the whole house with the glory of God as a hundred and twenty disciples were filled with the Spirit (Acts 2:1-4). This parallels the initial dedication of Solomon's temple, when the cloud of the divine presence filled the place (2 Chronicles 5:13-14) and fire fell on the altar (7:1-3) so that no priest or worshipper could stay on his feet.

Haggai's prophecy indicates a future visitation of the Spirit, to be as sudden as its earlier counterpart (compare Malachi 3:1), in a fulness of glory that will surpass the experience of the day of Pentecost (Haggai 2:3, 7, 9). This is the end-time revival for which we long.

3. Sluice-gate opened – mass Jewish ingrafting

In Romans 11:25-27 Paul predicts a wholesale ingathering of Jews into the kingdom at the end of this age. He quotes Isaiah 59:20-21, but with the deliberate alteration of one word: 'The deliverer,' he says, 'will come *from* Zion' (not '*to* Zion', as Isaiah originally said).

Zion here is not, of course, the Middle Eastern city of Jerusalem but spiritual Jerusalem, the church (Galatians 4:24-26; Hebrews 12:22-24). Paul is referring to the fulness of the present, largely Gentile phase of church history (Romans 11:11-12, 25). Christ, displayed in the vibrant life of the church, is going to touch the hard hearts of Jewish people and win them to himself. Jews will be converted on a grand scale.

This is portrayed for us in Isaiah 59, the source of Paul's quotation. Here we see the corporate Christ – the church – in the full armour of God (v16-17 in the light of Ephesians 6:10-18) 'come *to* Zion [Jewish people], to those in Jacob who repent of their sins' (v20). Christ's coming in revival will be 'like a pent-up flood that the breath [Spirit] of the Lord drives along' (v19).

The nineteenth-century evangelist Charles Finney, who knew revival from many first-hand experiences, reckoned: 'God is himself one pent-up revival.' When the river's sluice-gate is opened, Jews and Gentiles alike will discover 'life from the dead' (Romans 11:15) – revival indeed!

4. Subdued enemies – then the death-blow to death

In Romans 15:7-12 Paul quotes four Old Testament passages foretelling widespread Gentile conversion to Christ. This will be 'to confirm the promises made to the patriarchs' that 'in your seed all families of the earth will be blessed'.

His final quotation comes from Isaiah 11 (v10). In that passage, Isaiah promised that the Spirit of the Lord upon Messiah (v1-3a) would enable him to bring a just resolution to disputes between people of all nations (v3b-4a). This is described poetically in terms of his bringing 'lamb' and 'wolf', 'calf' and 'lion' into harmony, and neutralising Satan's venom (v6-9a; see also 1 John 3:8). Here is a picture of salvation blessings bringing peace and harmony within the Gentile world.

But, as we have seen, Jews are not to be strangers to these blessings. Isaiah explains that, just as God first called natural Israel out of Egypt (11:16), so he will gather Jews 'a second time' (v11) from every part of the earth into his kingdom, where they, too, will live in harmony (v10-16).

The worldwide peace and harmony to be achieved by the corporate Christ (v4b-5a; see also Ephesians 6:10-18) will come about not by force of arms but by the preaching of the gospel. This is described as 'the rod of his mouth', 'the sword of the Spirit' which is the utterance (Greek *rhema*) of God (compare Revelation 19:11-16; Hebrews 4:12). The success of the message will lie in its proclamation in the anointing of the Spirit (Isaiah 11:1-3).

Psalm 110, much quoted in the New Testament, conveys the same message. Although David probably composed this poem for Solomon's coronation, his prayer will find ultimate fulfilment only in the reign of his later descendant, the great King Jesus. And the fulfilment is not to be in some future utopian millennium, but in this present age, as he extends his rule among his enemies.

Christ sat down at the right hand of God at his ascension, since when 'he waits for his enemies to be made his footstool' (Hebrews 10:12-13). The destruction of these enemies is a process, taking place now as the message of the kingdom increases in its influence, though the final enemy, death, will be destroyed only when Jesus comes again from heaven (1 Corinthians 15:25-26).

Legally, God has already placed everything under Christ's feet – and that means under our feet, as his body (Ephesians 1:22). It simply needs working out in practice. And that need not take a long time; he can suddenly ('soon', Romans 16:20) crush Satan under our feet. He will do this when we, his people, volunteer freely as we are invigorated with the reviving dew of the Spirit's presence 'in the day of [his] power' (Psalm 110:3 NASB).

Then the last Adam – Christ and his church, Head and body together – will complete the original commission to 'fill the earth and subdue it' (Genesis 1:28, Hebrew 'tread down'). All nations will be discipled by God's commandments issuing from the church, God's house (Isaiah 2:2-4; Matthew 28:18-20).

Sudden glory is the longing of our hearts as we seek to see the fulfilment in our time of these Old Testament prophecies concerning revival.

NOTES

1. I hold to the view that Christ's victory, won definitively at his death, resurrection and ascension, will be worked out in history during this present age – end-time revival included – as his enemies are made his footstool. I therefore reject the pessimistic premillennial view that the church will end up in a 'Laodicean' phase, lacking in zeal and smug about its unrevived condition.

2. *Manners and Customs in Bible Lands,* by F.H. Wight, Moody Press, Chicago, Illinois, 1979

The New Testament basis for revival hope

Tony Ling

The apostolic writers were no pessimists. They saw the triumph of Christ's kingdom in a mighty end-time harvest

Contrary to nature, unsupported by past experience and impossible in the present circumstances. Those were the facts. But this was God's word, his plan that had been revealed – and by an angel at that! The Son of the Most High was coming, he had said, to occupy David's throne and to rule over an everlasting kingdom.

Not that the appearance of the promised Messiah posed a problem to her. Like others of the faithful remnant, she had longed and prayed for that day. And the expectation of the kingdom of God burned brightly in the aspirations of her heart.

No, her confusion was not in the *purpose* – but in the *process*. For she, Mary – a virgin – was to give birth to the Son of God. No wonder the question filling her mind and tumbling from her mouth was, 'How will this be?'

In answer, the angel Gabriel brought a revelation of how *all* the 'impossible' purposes of God are caused to prosper:

'The Holy Spirit will come upon you, and the power of the Most High will overshadow you' (Luke 1:26-35).

God's intervention

The progress of God's eternal plan, apparently pedestrian at times, is at other times dynamically and dramatically advanced by divine intervention and Holy Spirit visitation.

The Old Testament is full of prophetic promise and historic example of this principle. Men like Zerubbabel learned by word and experience that the work of God is founded and finished, that mountains of unclimbable obstruction are transformed into plains of easy access, not by human might and power, ' "but by my Spirit," says the Lord Almighty' (Zechariah 4:6).

If old covenant saints, who without us could not be made perfect, experienced great and gracious seasons of visitation, how much more should we, who are partakers of a better covenant founded upon better promises? In fact, most of the old covenant promises are actually for the new covenant people.

Day and days

One important example beautifully illustrates this. At the end of the book of Amos, God makes this remarkable promise: 'The days are coming . . . when the reaper will be overtaken by the ploughman and the planter by the one treading grapes' (Amos 9:13).

The Lord speaks of future days when a great escalation of ingathering will be experienced. Days when the process of sowing and reaping will merge into one continuous operation. Days of perpetual harvest. But when are those days to be?

Immediately preceding that promise is another: 'In that day I will restore David's fallen tent' (Amos 9:11).

That day of restoration was inaugurated by the coming of Jesus who, as Gabriel had assured Mary, would be given 'the throne of his father David' (Luke 1:32). And the *day* of restoration was to be followed by *days* of revival. The church of the New Testament understood these verses from Amos as proof of a worldwide move of the Holy Spirit to gather men and women from every nation into the church of Jesus Christ (Acts 15:13-18).

The risen Christ had instructed his disciples that the enduement of power from on high would equip them to be effective witnesses to the ends of the earth. The day of Pentecost itself furnished them with an eloquent demonstration of this when, in a moment of time, 'devout men from every nation under heaven' heard and responded to the word of God.

In his message that day Peter explained: 'In the last *days*, God says, I will pour out my Spirit on all people . . . The sun will be turned to darkness and the moon to blood before the coming of the great and glorious *day* of the Lord' (Acts 2:17-21).

Notice once more the interaction between 'days' and 'day'. The whole cosmic purpose of God will be consummated in one 'great and glorious day'. But that day is to be preceded by days in which God has promised to pour out his Spirit upon all people.

Time to restore

Peter made that point again after the healing of the lame man at the temple gate. 'Repent,' he commanded the people, '. . . that your sins may be wiped out, that *times of refreshing* may come from the Lord.' And then, speaking of the promised second coming of Christ, he explained, 'He must remain in heaven until *the time comes for God to restore everything*' (Acts 3:19-21).

The universal recovery programme of God, inaugurated

at the coming of his Son into the world, reaches its glorious completion when Jesus comes again. But the time of ultimate restoration is itself the climax of countless times of refreshing.

The early disciples did not rely exclusively on their initial Holy Spirit baptism at Pentecost. It was a glorious beginning, but still only the beginning. New departures would require new demonstrations. Threatening antagonism demanded a fresh anointing.

So, in Acts 4, we discover their heart cry and heaven's response – physical shaking, spiritual filling, bold declaration, powerful demonstration – as God again intervened with a Holy Spirit visitation.

Harvests before the harvest

But it is not only the Acts of the Apostles that gives strong confirmation to the idea of revival being a major means of kingdom expansion. The earthly ministry of Jesus provides further examples.

In his parables of the kingdom, Jesus often used an agricultural analogy. The parable of the weeds, which he explained in detail to the disciples (Matthew 13:24-30, 36-43), portrays 'the end of the age' as the ultimate harvest – the gathering up of both the righteous and the wicked.

As Acts shows us that 'the day' is preceded by 'days', and 'the time' by 'times', it is not surprising to find Jesus talking of harvests before the harvest. Remember, Amos had spoken of unseasonal harvests in the days to come – and Jesus produced them! If the disciples were accustomed to saying, 'Four months more and then the harvest', Jesus heightened their expectation and hastened the day by declaring, 'Look at the fields! They are ripe for harvest' (John 4:35).

What was true at that time in Samaria was also true in Judea. 'The harvest is plentiful but the workers are few,' Jesus said. 'Ask the Lord of the harvest, therefore, to send out workers into his harvest field' (Matthew 9:37-38).

Sometimes, it seems, the need is not so much for God to produce a crop ripe for harvest, but for a people of discerning spirit to see it and of dedicated heart to reap it.

Divine precedent

Since the day of his ascension, Jesus has punctuated the history of his church with sovereign acts of revival. Most of us have read about them and longed for them. But can we legitimately expect them?

Charles Spurgeon said, 'What he has done once is a prophecy of what he intends to do again. Whatever God has done in the way of converting sinners is to be looked upon as a precedent.' It seems to me beyond question that the world is destined for a great and glorious revival in which multitudes will be swept into the kingdom of God.

John saw it like this: 'Before me was a white cloud, and seated on the cloud was one "like a son of man" with a crown of gold on his head and a sharp sickle in his hand. Then [an] angel came out of the temple and called in a loud voice to him who was sitting on the cloud, "Take your sickle and reap, because the time to reap has come, for the harvest of the earth is ripe." So he who was seated on the cloud swung his sickle over the earth, and the earth was harvested' (Revelation 14:14-16).

Jewish awakening

One great promised (and as yet unfulfilled) ingathering alone should be enough to enliven the confidence of our faith. In Romans 11, Paul alludes to a mighty move of God among the Jews. Not that they are somehow to supplant the church as God's people, but that they are to be grafted back into the original rootstock of God's holy covenants as part of his church. This will come about when 'the fulness of the Gentiles has come in' (v25 NASB).

In his commentary on Romans, John Murray says of this expression: 'The fulness of the Gentiles denotes unprecedented blessing on them, but does not exclude even greater blessings to follow.'[1]

Surely what we are seeing here is continual revivals of increasing magnitude among Gentiles, leading to a dynamic awakening among the Jews. And even that is not the end. For if Israel's loss was the means of the Gentiles' riches, how much greater riches will their fulness bring! If their rejection resulted in the reconciliation of the world, what will their acceptance be but life from the dead!

John Wesley's notes on Romans contain this comment: 'When [the salvation of Israel] is accomplished, it will be so strong a demonstration . . . as will doubtless convince many thousand [nominal Christians] . . . And this will be a means of swiftly propagating the gospel among [Muslims] and pagans.'[2]

The church came to birth in the fires of revival – and will come to its fulness in the midst of an even greater blaze of glory. The former rain produced the firstfruits; the latter rain will herald the harvest home. But in the time between, every generation in every nation must stir its own expectation of Holy Spirit visitation.

'Revive your work in the midst of the years!' (Habakkuk 3:2 RAV) must be the ceaseless prayer of the church of God.

NOTES

1.   *Commentary on Romans*, by John Murray, Eerdmans, 1968
2.   *Explanatory Notes Upon the New Testament*, by John Wesley, Epworth Press, 1976

A radical goal for radical Christians

David Mansell

If future revival is not to run up a cul-de-sac we will need to be more radical than our predecessors

We are looking, praying and working for world revival.

Anything less falls short of God's intention. Anything less will fail to bring in the kingdom and bring back the King. It would be a tragedy if this generation passed into history leaving behind only a memory and another book as an epitaph to a revival that came and went.

The main point of Jesus' last words to his disciples and the apostolic preaching in the early chapters of Acts was an explanation of how God intended the Pentecost revival, which brought the church to birth, to progress.

Revival would lead to greater revival. Beginning at Jerusalem, the fire would spread first to Judea, then to Samaria and then to the remotest parts of the earth (Acts 1:8).

The outpouring of the Spirit would be like the latter rain that swells the grain ready for harvest. There would be times and seasons, each time of refreshing rain being followed by another. Season would follow season just as spring and summer follow winter, and all would find their destiny in the autumn harvest.

Through these seasons of testimony to the Lord Jesus in all the earth, together with times of refreshing from heaven, God would restore to his people all that the prophets had promised. A time of repentance, turning to the Lord, refreshing and restoration would engulf the entire world so that God could send the Christ, the anointed King from heaven, to claim his inheritance (Acts 3:19-21).

The revival that God has promised is a coming of the Spirit that abides, a move of God that keeps moving, an outpouring that continues till the world is filled with the knowledge of the Lord.

A call for radical Christians

The story of revival is both thrilling and sad. Thrilling to see what God can do when he breaks into people's lives, sad to see how every wave of revival so far has finally spent its energy on the beach of religious self-interest.

Where future revival leads will depend very much on where we want it to lead. If it is to bring God's purpose for this world to its appointed conclusion, *we will need to be more radical than our predecessors.*

Revival is like a flood. It will not run in the channels cut by our preferences, prejudices and traditions. When it comes, it overwhelms, invades, takes over and sweeps away all that lies before it.

It is no use preparing a way for the Lord by prayer and humbling ourselves if, when he comes, he finds the route full of road-blocks and diversions to protect our private lives, personal hobby-horses and denominational entrenchments. God will never revive a fence. He will never revive what he has sentenced to die.

In revival, there is a dying as well as a bringing to birth. The chaff burns while the wheat is gathered into the barn.

Being radical is not an end in itself; it is allowing God to do with us what he likes, when he likes and as often as he likes.

Being radical is removing now what God himself will remove, and doing now what God himself will do when he breaks in with revival.

What are we waiting for? If we really want what revival will surely bring to the world, why not let it begin in us today?

Divine breakthrough

I once read in a church report on a two-week evangelistic outreach: 'Nobody was saved but the saints were encouraged.'

The revival we are looking for will do more than encourage the saints! A glance at an atlas of world religions shows that, after two thousand years of gospel preaching, billions are still totally unaffected. The Bible tells us to expect the following areas of breakthrough in revival:

1. The gospel preached

The gospel will be preached worldwide in such a way as to challenge every ideology, expose every false religion and undermine every society based on evil, corruption and injustice.

In their place will arise the community of the redeemed, having the glory of God. Justice, love and racial harmony will spring like a fountain from hearts washed clean by the blood of Jesus and empowered by the abiding presence of the Holy Spirit.

2. True unity

Unity of those who truly own Jesus as Lord will be a prominent feature. No ecumenism, no compromise, no cosmetic gestures, just one heart, one mind and one soul for Jesus.

3. Outpouring on Israel

There will be a mighty outpouring of the Spirit on the nation of Israel. Its magnitude and effect on the world are described as 'life from the dead' (Romans 11:15).

4. Islamic nations turn to Christ

Isaiah prophesied, 'In that day there will be a highway from Egypt to Assyria. The Assyrians will go to Egypt and the Egyptians to Assyria. The Egyptians and Assyrians will worship together. In that day Israel will be the third, along with Egypt and Assyria, a blessing on the earth. The Lord God Almighty will bless them, saying, "Blessed be Egypt my people, Assyria my handiwork, and Israel my inheritance" ' (Isaiah 19:23-25).

5. Demonic powers overthrown

Again it was Isaiah who prophesied, 'In that day the Lord will punish the powers in the heavens above and the kings on the earth below' (Isaiah 24:21).

Demons achieve their evil ends by controlling the hearts of men in general (John 13:27) and kings in particular (Daniel 10:13). They are the powers of this dark world, the spiritual forces of evil in the heavenly realms against whom we stand (Ephesians 6:12). They control the whole world system (Ephesians 2:2; Revelation 18:2, 23).

'The God of peace will soon crush Satan under your feet,' says Paul (Romans 16:20). The power of the Holy Spirit is the power to drive out evil spirits (Matthew 10:1; Mark 16:17). The evidence of the release from demonic strongholds will be striking. The whole realm of the occult will be exposed and lives set free from its snare. Heathen will be released from superstition to turn to Christ.

Society will be dramatically influenced. Drunkenness, addiction, homosexuality, fornication, blasphemy, greed, injustice and arrogance will be dealt a mighty blow as the spirit of repentance moves from community to community, town to town and nation to nation.

6. Nations turning to Christ

The Bible envisages times of national breaking in of God's Spirit (for example, Zechariah 12:11 – 13:2). In the days of Jonah the entire city of Nineveh turned to the Lord (Jonah 3:1-10). Again, we read in Acts 9:35, 'All those who lived in Lydda and Sharon saw [Aeneas, the paralytic man who had been healed] and turned to the Lord.'

Imagine the social impact: everyone in the town born again! Imagine this happening across nations throughout the world!

The presence of God

'Oh, that you would rend the heavens and come down,' prayed the prophet (Isaiah 64:1). Revival is *the coming of God himself.* The prophet is sent only to prepare the way for the Lord to presence himself personally among his people – a presence that will achieve what the ministry can never achieve, be it ever so anointed.

Luke observes that, in the early days of the outpouring of the Holy Spirit, 'everyone was filled with awe' (Acts 2:43). This has characterised every revival since.

'The Holy Ghost descended on us; not indeed "as a rushing mighty wind", yet as the gentle zephyr, till it filled the whole place. So powerful was the influence that none of us could speak for some minutes. We all gave vent to our feelings in floods of joyful tears.'[1]

When God draws near, there is a deep sense of the reality of divine things and a need to be right with God, a seriousness yet a lightness of spirit that overwhelms the heart.

Such awareness is experienced not only in meetings but also in the street, driving the car or in a restaurant. Suddenly, God draws near and one is almost overpowered with the awareness of it. When revival comes, we expect this presence to abide on every heart and in every home where Christ is owned as Lord.

So powerful is the effect of this divine presence that sinners are seized with conviction and converted to Christ.

'What I felt, apart from what I saw, convinced me at once that this was no ordinary movement. I have known men out in the fields so overcome by this sense of God that they were found prostrate on the ground. Here are the words of one who felt the hand of God upon him: "The grass beneath my feet and rocks around me seemed to cry, 'Flee to Christ for refuge.' " '2

The judgment of God

God's nearness, besides being felt as an awesome presence, is sometimes manifest during times of revival in *acts of judgment*. Ananias and Sapphira were the first to fall down dead for lying to the Holy Spirit (Acts 5:1-11).

'At a village in North Wales there was a young man who, though young, had become so hardened as to laugh at the tears and prayers of his pious mother. One evening in the first week of last month he stood outside the window of the village chapel to mock the good people who were holding a prayer meeting there.

'An elderly woman seeing him, rebuked him, but his insolent reply was, "Go, you, and serve your Master and let me alone to serve mine."

'A few minutes after, he was found lying in the road, with his face to the ground. A person happening to pass raised him up, and having recognised him inquired what ailed him.

' "I do not know," he said, "unless God is about to kill me; I am very ill."

'His sickness, however, was "not unto death", but "for the glory of God". He was taken home and laid on the bed. For some days he suffered the most dreadful mental agony but at length found peace in believing; and this mocker is now one of the most earnest men of prayer in the village.'[3]

Angelic appearances

The Bible speaks of 'signs and wonders'. Sometimes these were miracles of healing, while at other times the veil was drawn back so that what is normally invisible to the natural eye became visible: *angels appeared.*

Jesus' first coming was attended by angelic manifestations. An angel appeared both to Mary (Luke 1:26-27) and to Joseph (Matthew 1:20). When the day of Jesus' birth came, 'suddenly a great company of the heavenly host appeared with the angel, praising God' (Luke 2:10-14).

Angelic appearances and heavenly singing occur in times of revival.

In the 1859 revival Evan Jones describes a meeting in which 'A heavenly sound was heard in the song of praise . . . The song of praise continued for more than forty minutes without interruption'.[4]

The same phenomenon occurred at the Dales Bible Week in 1977. On several evenings after the meeting was over and the auditorium vacated and locked up for the night, heavenly singing was heard coming from the building at two or three o'clock in the morning. This was not only reported by those on site; people living in the houses near the site complained about the singing in the early hours of the morning!

During the same week there were several angelic appearances, particularly to the young. One six-year-old boy, lost in the crowd and anxiously awaited by his parents, suddenly turned up full of smiles. When asked how he found his way he replied, 'Oh, a nice ghost in a shiny coat showed me the way.'

During a time of testimony another lad of six was asked what he enjoyed most about the Bible Week. He replied, 'I liked it best when all the angels came and flew round the children's meeting playing their trumpets and praising God.'

Divine direction

In revival we look for the progress of the gospel to be marked by *divine direction and attestation*. Examples are found throughout the book of Acts:

☐ A vision directing Peter to Cornelius (10:1-48; 11:4-15)

☐ A prophetic word separating Paul and Barnabas (13:1-52)

☐ Doors shut in Asia and Bithynia but a visitation directing Paul to Macedonia (16:6-10)

☐ The confirmation that Paul should continue in Corinth without fear of his persecutors (18:9-11)

☐ Warnings to Paul about what would take place as he went to Jerusalem (20:22-24)

As the apostles went forth into all the world at the Lord's command, they avoided wasted time by moving at the direction of the Holy Spirit. We are looking for that same clarity.

I remember hearing Willie Burton describe how he was called with others to go to the Congo (now Zaïre). As they waited on God, they were given, through prophecy, the names of the towns where they were to go. They had heard none of the strange-sounding names before, but when they checked the map, there they were, just as God had said.

The result was hundreds of churches planted in the power of the Holy Spirit.

Works of power

In revival we can expect *mighty works of power*. Jesus said, 'Anyone who has faith in me will do what I have been doing.

He will do even greater things than these, because I am going to the Father' (John 14:12).

We look to see more than just some healings in our meetings. As at the beginning, we will expect signs and wonders as a divine attestation that we are working in the right place. Too often the mission has closed just as God has started to work.

I was once at a church for a week's meetings. On the second night God told me, 'I want to heal the sick.' By the last evening people were coming a hundred miles to the meetings and we were seeing miracles, including a man who came in paralysed but pushed his wheelchair out of the door at the end.

I often wonder what would have happened if we had allowed God to continue, instead of sticking to the diary – particularly as the next place I visited was totally dead and nothing happened! In order for us to reach the world, our diaries will need to change to suit God's plans.

It is healings that often produce the breakthrough we look for. I remember being in Africa with Bryn Jones. The first meeting was hard going.

'We need a breakthrough of the power of God to open this lot up,' I whispered to Bryn.

'Well, let's get on with it,' he replied.

Standing before the gathering I declared, 'God wants to show his hand in power here this afternoon. Will those who are sick and want God to heal them come forward.'

About six out of six hundred trickled to the front. First in line was a truck driver with disintegrating vertebrae in his neck, wearing a surgical collar. He had been like it for nine years. He was instantly healed, tore off his collar, turned his neck and touched his toes.

Shouts filled the place and hundreds surged forward, many of them Muslims and spirit-worshippers. Everyone who came for healing was healed, and many were saved, delivered from demons and filled with the Holy Spirit.

We expect the powers of darkness to be dispossessed when
the power of the Lord is present to heal. We expect the power
of God to fall on entire companies and even communities.
We expect demons to fear when the servants of the Lord come
to town.

Realising our destiny

Destiny implies destination. To speak of ourselves as a people
of destiny *we must know where we are going*.

Duncan Campbell wrote, 'How many today are really
prepared to face the stark fact that we have been
outmanoeuvred by the strategy of hell because we have tried
to meet the enemy on human levels by human strategy? In
this we may have succeeded in making people church-
conscious, mission-conscious or even crusade-conscious,
without making them God-conscious.'[5]

Our destiny is to bring God-consciousness to a God-
oblivious world, and we do it best when we stop trying too
hard and are conscious only of the presence of God abiding
with us.

When John the Baptist cried, 'Look, the Lamb of God,'
it was not to make a dramatic point in his sermon, but because he saw Jesus literally approaching (John 1:29).

'Look . . . I see heaven open and the Son of Man standing
at the right hand of God,' cried Stephen as, full of the Holy
Spirit, he gazed into heaven and saw the glory of God (Acts
7:54-60). God himself had opened heaven and broken in to
make the final appeal! The hearers were cut to the heart as
they found themselves standing in the presence of a man
standing in the presence of God.

The Lewis revival in north-west Scotland saw this same
drawing power of God's presence among his people. As the
little group seeking revival experienced the coming of the
Holy Spirit in the middle of the night, they opened the door
of the building where they were meeting to discover that a

crowd had gathered. God had brought conviction of sin upon the townspeople one by one and each made his way from his bed to the place of prayer to seek the Lord.

As we trim our lamps, we will be the light to the world (Matthew 25:7).

As we in all things grow up into him, Jesus will fill the world (Ephesians 4:15).

As we are brought to complete unity, it will let the world know that Jesus was sent (John 17:23).

As we give room for the Holy Spirit to work in our gatherings, the unbeliever will fall down and exclaim, 'God is really among you!' (1 Corinthians 14:24-25).

As we walk in victory, the fragrance of the knowledge of Christ will spread everywhere (2 Corinthians 2:14).

As our hearts become the tablets on which the Spirit writes God's laws, so we will become a letter from Christ, known and read by everybody (2 Corinthians 3:2).

As we go forth into all the world, so Jesus will go with us and work till the job is done (Matthew 28:19-20).

Revival will lead us to the fulfilment of our destiny – and all creation waits in eager expectation for this time when the sons of God will be revealed (Romans 8:19).

NOTES

1. *The Welsh Revival,* by Thomas Phillips, Banner of Truth, 1989

2. *God's Answer – Revival Sermons,* by Duncan Campbell, Faith Mission, Edinburgh, 1960

3. Phillips, op. cit.

4. *The 1859 Revival in Ireland,* by W.E. Allen, Revival Publishing Company, Belfast, 1955

5. *In the Day of Thy Power,* by Arthur Wallis, Christian Literature Crusade, London, 1956

Revival and the mature man

David Matthew

*One day, the body of Christ must match the glory
of the Head*

As a rule we tend to use female terms for the church, seeing
her as the bride of Christ, preparing herself for her husband
(Ephesians 5:25-27; Revelation 21:2, 9). But no one word-
picture is sufficient to portray every aspect, and so Paul, in
Ephesians 4:13, describes the end-time church as *andra teleion*
– 'a mature man' (NASB).

Such a description no more fits today's worldwide church
than does that of the spotless bride. Both pictures envisage
the church as it will ultimately be, prior to Christ's return.
And we must keep those pictures in mind, because our
convictions about the church's future will dictate how we act
now, how we relate to other Christians today, how we view
the current ecclesiastical scene.

Those convictions are also crucial to the revival question.
There can be no separating the issue of a great ingathering
of souls from that of the church into which those souls are
to be gathered.

Indeed, the same holds true in non-revival times. Chris and

Sue Brown, describing their struggles in an inner-city church, wrote: 'Had we seen many converts at that time, it is doubtful whether we could have held them. A friend said, "All our evangelism is like an arm beckoning, 'Come', but there is no body to come to." '[1]

Someone has likened much local church evangelism to 'fishing from a boat with a hole in its hull'. To change the image, what is the point of calling lost sinners out of the wind and rain into a drab and chilly house whose structure is so flimsy that the whole building could collapse on their heads at any moment?

'The time has come,' said Peter, 'for judgment to begin at the house of God' (1 Peter 4:17 RAV). Most of us want blessing, but not judgment. Usually, when we cry for the presence of the Lord to be known more keenly among us, we have a limited view of what that means. We are crying for power, miracles and vigorous spiritual life. But the presence of the Lord in blessing cannot be separated from his presence in judgment, because he is holy. What if his presence were to bring an Ananias and Sapphira situation?

As churches come into line with God's will, the irrigation channels are dug to take the revival rain when it comes. Conversely, every touch of revival is intended to challenge our church life, prodding it in the direction of the 'mature man' into which it must ultimately grow.

What is the church?

At this point we must pause to ask that most crucial of questions: What do we mean by 'the church'? Broadly speaking, there are three possible answers:

1. The mystical body of Christ

Sometimes called 'the invisible church', this is *the sum total of all born-again believers, past, present and future* – all whose names are in the Lamb's book of life, chosen in Christ before the foundation of the world.

Many members of that body have, of course, already departed this life and are now with Christ. But they are one with those alive on earth, and even with those, still unsaved, who are yet to enter their Christian calling.

This view of the church emphasises the 'mystical' oneness, the spiritual link which binds together the many members separated by time and space. Only after Christ's return will the invisible become visible.

Such a concept of the church is legitimate, but its obvious danger is the dismissal of any possibility of *outward* oneness and maturity this side of glory. Adherents of this school of thought settle easily for the visible church's imperfections. Their future expectation tends to provoke little change in local church life since only the return of Christ, they believe, can bring the church to its goal.

2. The institutional church

The world is littered with denominational and institutional wineskins. They fall into two broad categories.

Some (like the Roman Catholic Church, the Church of England and the Methodist Church) are 'mixture' churches. In most, infant baptism ensures a steady influx of members who remain nominal in their Christianity. A living experience of Christ in new birth is not a requirement for membership – it is enough to attend services or sacraments from time to time and voice acceptance of the church's credal basis.

Others (like Pentecostal churches and the Brethren) are 'gathered' churches, insisting on a clear conversion experience, evidenced by a changed life, as the ground of membership.

Seeing it against this background, some regard 'church' as *the sum total of all these denominational streams*.

On this view, all that is required to produce unity is to dig channels from one stream to another so that they all merge into one institutional river. The World Council of Churches is the biggest trench-digger. But even if it succeeds in bringing about the ultimate merger, the one river will not be the church at all in the scriptural sense, because it will contain many who are not Christians by biblical definition.

Some believe the denominational streams can be purified and that the charismatic renewal is the cleansing agent. As the institutional churches are individually purged, the eventual one big river will, they believe, run clean, and so the 'mature man' will emerge.

The theory is attractive, but in practice it doesn't work. The institutions are inherently resistant to change. A degree of renewal might occur. Slow modifications may take place in some aspects of denominational life and structure. But experience – including the experience of revival, when change is most easy – shows that, unless the institutional structure is voluntarily dismantled, one of two things happens. Either the flame of renewal is doused or the renewed individuals escape for their lives and start again outside.

3. The redeemed community

The context of Paul's 'mature man' teaching is an earthly one. Gifted leaders are pictured moving among the believers, building them up, teaching them how to serve and how to resist the winds of wrong doctrine. This is a picture of the church here below. The departed saints are with Christ in heaven, beyond the need of such things.

The church is here viewed, then, as *the sum total of believers on earth at any one time*. Some might call themselves Baptists, Salvationists, Catholics or a score of other names. Others would repudiate any such non-biblical titles and claim to be 'just Christians'. But one thing they have in common: their names are written in heaven, and that uniting factor outweighs all their differences. Over the heart of each one is stamped 'Redeemed . . . by the precious blood of Christ'.

Seeds of manhood

It is this redeemed population – a shifting population, for there is a constant flow of some going to glory and others being newly converted – who are destined to emerge as Paul's 'mature man'.

Already they are joined in a mystical union. But since maturity and visible unity are inseparable (Ephesians 4:13), we must expect what is purely mystical to become increasingly outward and practical. For that to happen, the redeemed community (singular) on earth must form itself into redeemed communities (plural) – local churches where God's purposes can be worked out without hindrance.

In such churches, local elders will care for the people with godly simplicity. Each believer, finding his place in the local body, will be thereby equipped to be salt and light in society at large. Apostles, prophets, evangelists, shepherds and teachers will move among the churches to strengthen them and impart the wisdom of God (see Ephesians 4:11-13).

These churches will choose to live in the enjoyment of *all* the truths of the New Testament, and will be flexible in adapting to the wind of the Spirit as he bends them this way or that. They will be ready for revival. And as individual local churches develop in this manner, so the church worldwide will begin to take on the shape of maturity.

The mature man must emerge as a robust and wholesome church. We shall see in every nation on earth, in every city, town and village, companies of believers living in the good of all that God originally intended.

Like any mature man, they will be strong and decisive yet kind and considerate, above the petty squabblings of immature youth. They will demonstrate godly authority, firm conviction (the 'unity in the faith', Ephesians 4:13) and quiet power. In short, they will be like Jesus.

A body fit for the Head

At present the redeemed community is a pathetic parody of

the 'mature man'. Its Head is the glorious, risen Christ, perfect in kingly splendour. He sits enthroned on high while, like some monstrous deformity of childbirth, his body, the church, is dwarfed and puny, totally out of keeping with such a glorious Head.

Even so, 'he is not ashamed to call them brothers' (Hebrews 2:11). What a desire should be ours, therefore, to grow up into 'the whole measure of the fulness of Christ' (Ephesians 4:13), to 'grow up into him who is the Head' (v15)! Jesus deserves nothing less.

The weary world, too, deserves nothing less. The major hindrance to revival is the church. Like ancient Israel, the church is meant to be 'a light to the Gentiles'. Instead, it hears the Judge's awful assessment: 'God's name is blasphemed among the Gentiles because of you' (Romans 2:24). There is nothing wrong with Jesus; it is the church bearing his name that puts people off him. That's why local churches must change.

One day soon, body and Head must match, and there is much we can do now to hasten the matching. The church on earth must become a fitting body for its perfect Head, the two together forming that spiritual giant – Head in heaven and body on earth – which will dominate society. Its growth in quality will be the trigger for revival; its growth in quantity will be the result of revival. The 'mature man' at last!

I say again, your expectations for the future must dictate your actions today. The emergence of the 'mature man' has to be not only sighed for but also worked for. What changes, then, do you need to be making now?

Read again Ephesians 4:1-16. Catch a glimpse of the glorious church it portrays and alter course accordingly.

NOTES

1. Chris & Sue Brown, *City Vineyard – A church bears fruit in inner London*, Harvestime, Bradford, 1989

Suddenly all heaven broke loose!

Bryn Jones

One man's vision of the coming revival

Evangelical Christianity today is experiencing amazing
numerical growth around the world. In several third world
countries the rate of conversion exceeds that of population
growth.

Yet despite numerical growth, there can only be
disappointment with the appalling lack of spiritual depth.
In many cases spiritual realities have been sacrificed to
religious expediency and the righteousness of God devalued
to accommodate human weakness.

The next revival will inevitably require a radical revolution.
Isaiah saw this and said, 'The proud look of man will be
abased, and the loftiness of man will be humbled, and the
Lord alone will be exalted in that day' (Isaiah 2:11 NASB).
There must be an overthrowing of all that is the result of
man's ego so that what Christ has built may be seen. God
intends to destroy all that is contrary to his divine purpose
and to bring about his intended goal of a united church filled
with his glory.

Examination of past revivals reveals recurring patterns in the renewal of spiritual life. Webster's Dictionary defines renewal as 'to make life new; restore to freshness, vigour or perfection; to make new spiritually'.

Revivals have always brought renewal in prayer, in love for the Word of God, in righteousness, in joy, in witness and in praise and worship.

A striking vision

Many of these features combined in a personal vision I received when a student at Bible college. It has deeply affected my life.

It was the usual morning chapel hour before the start of a day of lectures. That day, however, was not turning out to be 'the usual'. Across the room, students and staff alike were falling to their knees before God. A deep sense of his presence was among us. I lay prostrate before him, crying out in prayer that what we were experiencing at that moment would continue and intensify until the church of God worldwide felt the power of his presence.

Suddenly all heaven broke loose! I found myself caught up in the Spirit, no longer conscious of a room full of people, but deeply aware of being granted audience with the King.

In a vision I saw great throngs of people, old and young alike, laughing and shouting, clapping, singing and praising as they moved along the roads. Everywhere they went they carried light into the darkness of their surroundings. Cripples were jumping up and walking, the blind were being prayed for on the streets and their eyes were opening. Industrial machinery was coming to a stop as workmen prayed and found the Lord. Shops were emptying of people, astonished at the miracles taking place in the streets.

All the time, the crowd kept getting larger, until it was a sea of people praising God. The light increased until I could see no darkness at all. Everything was alive and exciting, everybody was happy and the power of God was everywhere, heaven was everywhere!

I found myself praising God in tongues, increasing in volume, then subsiding, then singing with the spirit, then subsiding. Then, just as suddenly as I had been caught into the vision and trance, I was back in the room, praying among the others.

That evening as I walked in the college garden, an Ethiopian girl approached me and asked me how long I had spent in Eritrea. Mystified, I replied, 'I've never been there.'

She looked astonished, then told me that in the visitation that morning I had suddenly broken out in her native language – an Eritrean dialect – praising God for great signs, wonders and miracles that were taking place. I had also, she said, prophesied a great outpouring of God that would sweep the world and bring his glory into the streets.

As she spoke I trembled and wept, for I knew God the Holy Spirit had spoken. For the next three days I sought God's face in prayer and fasting and was taken by the Spirit into some of the deepest experiences of communion with God that I have ever known.

I was allowed in the Spirit a measure of understanding as to what Jesus had groaned and wept for; what he had seen in that cup in the Garden of Gethsemane; what was the true nature of the 'joy that was set before him' which enabled him to endure the cross. I was given a sense of God's great delight in fulfilling the travail of his soul so that he might see its outcome and be satisfied.

'How, Lord?'

What I saw that day in my spirit of the glory of the church of the final generation is as clear to me now as it was then, in spite of the passing years.

'Lord,' I remember crying, 'how can the church ever come into such glory? We are so divided, so defensive!'

The words that the Holy Spirit spoke in reply burn on in my heart: 'I will pour out my Spirit and I will restore.'

Since that time my understanding of the great intention of God in revival and restoration has increased. Peter said

that God would 'send Jesus, the Christ appointed for you,
whom heaven must receive until the period of restoration of
all things about which God spoke by the mouth of his holy
prophets from ancient time' (Acts 3:20-21 NASB).

The word 'restoration' in this context implies more than
a recovery of the original practice of the church. It goes
beyond that to God's original intention for the church, and
implies a pressing forward into everything included in that
intention.

A return of the church to its condition after Pentecost would
be at the same time both glorious and discouraging. Running
parallel to the great manifestations of God's power and glory
were the legalism of judaistic teaching, the divisive carnality
of the Corinthians and many other evident imperfections.

The restoration accompanying the end-time revival will
both renew us in what has *already* been restored of faith and
power, and also equip us with what is *yet to be* restored in
revelation, experience, government, authority and the power
of God.

Changed expectations

Any student of past revivals knows that, for the most part,
they have broken into generations that had largely abandoned
God. Such revivals have often come with the suddenness of
Paul's experience on the Damascus Road, but engulfing the
church rather than the individual.

This was the kind of revival I had been anticipating for
years in praying for a visitation of God's Spirit. My
expectation came as a result of being brought up, as a
Welshman, on stories of the Welsh Revival of 1904-5 –
dramatic accounts of overnight change in the life of whole
towns and villages. But many of the chapels and churches
in those places had now been virtually empty for years, like
the dying embers of burnt-out volcanoes. I expected revival
to bring a sudden filling again.

This expectation was radically changed during that

experience of corporate intercession back in 1961. As we lay on our faces, overwhelmed by the presence and power of God's Spirit, I had a vision of the hills of Wales with gentle, drizzling rain falling over them. I looked intently at what I was seeing, expecting the drizzle to yield to a torrential downpour. But the vision did not change: the steady drizzle continued.

I am uncertain as to how long the vision continued, but in my spirit I was aware that what I was seeing represented a prolonged period of time. There was neither let-up nor increase in the intensity of the drizzle. Yet as I watched, the little streams tumbling down the mountains slowly became rivers that swelled and increased as they flowed through the valleys until throughout the small towns of the valleys there were areas of flooding.

I realised that God was saying an astonishing thing: *The coming spiritual visitation will be not so much a torrential downpour as a steady and continuous visitation of the Holy Spirit.* And it will have a greater and more lasting impact than any that has gone before.

I could not help comparing what I was seeing of God's visitation to the church with his visitation in the person of Jesus to a generation of two thousand years ago. He came as an unnoticed baby, not as a king in pomp and ceremony. He came to an obscure village and an obscure family, not to Jerusalem or the king's palace. He lived for thirty years as God fully expressed in a man without any public recognition of the fact!

Then the time came when he emerged into public view and a movement of God began among the people that caused the streams of expectation to grow into rivers of fulfilment. Yet even in the midst of all that, he wept over the people of Jerusalem for their failure to see what was taking place in their time. He spoke of a coming judgment that would devastate the city, leaving not one stone upon another. This, he said, was 'because you did not recognise the time of your visitation' (Luke 19:41-45 NASB).

Already, for those who have eyes to see, there are the
gathering clouds that signify coming rains. Indeed, many who
are holding out their hands and turning their faces heaven-
ward are beginning to feel gentle, fine raindrops. From many
parts of the world news continues to come in of a quiet yet
distinct growth of spiritual hunger and expectation. Cities
– even countries – that for years have been in deep spiritual
darkness are beginning to find light shining ever more brightly
in their midst.

The coming awakening, then, will not be like some sudden
tropical downpour that soon stops, only for everything quickly
to dry out again. I believe we are even now in the beginnings
of what will be a sustained visitation of God on a global scale,
visiting the elect of every nation. It will glorify God among
his people and prepare the church for the coming of the King
of kings.

Church of the supernatural

As I continued prostrate before the Lord, the vision of the
hills and rain quietly faded away, like a photographic slide
dissolving on a screen, only to give way to the emerging of
a new picture.

This was a scene of vast crowds and movement of people.
Everywhere I looked there were thousands of excited, happy
people praising God. There was laughter and much happy
talking and shouting, like some giant outdoor festival. It
reminded me of the street parties we had throughout Britain
for the coronation of Queen Elizabeth II.

The focus of the people's attention was the events taking
place in the streets of busy towns and cities. I watched
intently; there was no sign of meetings in public buildings,
with 'healing lines'. Instead, ordinary people were laying
hands on the sick in the streets and incredible miracles were
taking place.

No-one was going away sick. The crippled were getting
out of wheelchairs, blind people were instantly receiving their

sight, the deaf and dumb were finding they could hear and speak. And many of them were not even being prayed for; they were experiencing miracles without the visible involvement of others.

Prosperity ousts poverty

While I watched all this I became conscious of the lack of poverty among these happy people. 'Where,' I found myself asking, 'are the poor?'

Instantly my spirit received the response of the Spirit's voice: 'I will restore *all things.*' Then I realised that the restoration would be not only of things we count spiritual. It would be a practical expression of God's glory in the healing of the sick and the financial and material well-being of his people.

The absence of any special buildings was explained to me, in the Spirit, as signifying that the visitation of God will be on such a scale that what we have built as facilities for the church will no longer be able to contain the great harvest of God. The church of the supernatural will be an expression of Christ in the stream of daily life.

Although in the vision there were people praying for the sick, there weren't any significant figures catching everyone's attention – signifying that in that day of global visitation the Lord alone will be exalted.

People everywhere will be so Christ-centred and God-conscious that, whatever wonders men and women are doing, they will be seen only as servants of the Most High. Indeed, the involvement of the crowd in the praying suggested that it will the norm for *all* believers to operate in the realm of the supernatural.

Dark powers defeated

Once again the vision of crowds faded and a new picture emerged. This one was a scene of utter devastation. Great cities of the earth looked like decayed slums. Royal and presidential palaces, together with government buildings, were occupied by wasted figures, men and women with hopelessness written across their faces.

I became a listener to the conversations taking place in government committees and official bodies and was astonished at the lack-lustre proposals being presented. There was little sign of live debate. The approach seemed to be that, since no-one appeared to have any viable alternative proposals to offer, why bother opposing the ones already tabled?

This scene kept changing, allowing me to see not only into government bodies but also into religious, philosophical, educational, legal and scientific institutions. All of them were in a similar state of drab decay. The whole scene was of the last greys of twilight. Everything seemed to be dying, already wrapped in a shroud of darkness.

Surely, I thought, this is a picture of what the devil and his wicked spirits have done to the world. But the Holy Spirit broke abruptly into my thoughts with, 'No, this is what is happening to every institution finding its origin in man and representing an alternative to my kingdom. It is dying, not because the devil is destroying it, but *because the devil and his forces, who once motivated it, have been destroyed.*'

Then I realised that it was because of the emerging of the church of God in strength and glory, clothed with the supernatural power of the Holy Spirit, that the powers of darkness had been cast down. The sword of the Spirit, the word of God, was going out of the mouth of the believing church and destroying the works of the devil.

I understood then what 'the shaking of all things that can be shaken' really meant: 'His voice shook the earth, but now he has promised, "Once more I will shake not only the earth but also the heavens." The words "once more" indicate the removing of what can be shaken — that is, created things — so that what cannot be shaken may remain.

'Therefore, since we are receiving a kingdom that cannot be shaken, let us be thankful, and so worship God acceptably with reverence and awe, for our "God is a consuming fire" ' (Hebrews 12:26-29).

The same power of God that was making the church strong was also shaking the powers in the heavens, and earth's institutions and systems animated by them, so that only the kingdom of God with its unshakeable foundation would be seen to be of lasting worth.

Shining city

Again the picture dissolved, to be replaced by one of a strong city, bathed in bright light. I was aware in my spirit that this was the city pictured in the book of Revelation. What struck me was that it had now become the centre of attraction to the nations of the world.

There were streams of people coming across the globe towards the city, led by kings, presidents and other heads of state. As I looked closely, I saw hope written across their faces, as though they had just left situations of pressure and confusion which had reduced them to a state of despair. Now they seemed to be finding new hope as they streamed to the bright light of the City of God.

In my spirit I saw what this meant: the church of Jesus Christ, through the end-time visitation of the Holy Spirit, will be the only visible hope amid a crumbling and disintegrating society. The church will be viewed, not as the last hope of the despairing, but as the bright hope promising the fulfilment of all man's deepest desires.

The holy nation which is the church will be the 'mountain of the Lord's house, the highest of the mountains.' It will be the pinnacle of the nations and their source of hope. Such will be the manifestation of the power and presence of God that national leaders will come saying, 'Teach us the ways of God.' There will be a reaching out from every nation towards the City of God – the redeemed community.

Again I was made aware that they were not streaming to an individual but to a city. God was saying to me, 'It will not be to one spiritual figure heading up the church that they will turn. The answer to the final generation's dilemma lies in the church – the alternate society, a new and secure community amid the bankrupt society of the world.'

Gentle rains

And so, as this picture faded in its turn, there returned the original vision of the hills of Wales. The gentle, drizzling rain continued to fall.

The voice of the Spirit whispered in my soul, 'It will start gently and continue until the whole world drinks of its waters from heaven. Then men will suddenly awake to know that I am visiting my people, restoring my church in readiness for my appearing.'

As the vision came to an end I found myself weeping and sobbing, not in anguish but overwhelmed by deep joy and wonder. My heart was pounding. I felt as though my breath was being taken away, for I knew I was seeing God come in all his glory in the earth.

Today, whenever people say to me, 'History will only repeat itself. Whatever revival may come will eventually subside. This is the inevitable pattern of history and there's no breaking that pattern,' I remain unmoved, for I know that 'my eyes have seen the glory of the coming of the Lord'.

That great revival will *not* subside, for the King is coming to receive his Bride. How I long for that day when suddenly all heaven will break loose!

Part Three

Paving the way for revival – action now

'It is the around-the-corner brand of hope that prompts people to action, while the distant hope acts as opiate'

Eric Hoffer

Personal preparation for revival

Keri Jones

There are steps we can individually take to bring revival closer

It's a long time since, as a young Christian, I sat in my first prayer meeting for revival. But I well remember my thoughts at the time: 'If the effectiveness of the prayers is in proportion to the volume of the shouting and the copiousness of the tears, God must surely answer.'

But the meeting ended and people returned to their homes to continue life as before.

In due course I was to discover a sad fact: some of those same people, having fallen out, had not spoken to each other for several years! Their fervour for revival seemed undiminished, but it's hardly surprising that their prayers remained unanswered.

Passive or active?

Revival was always viewed by my friends and acquaintances as a sovereign move by God from heaven upon sinners who needed to be born again into new life in Jesus.

In line with this strong emphasis on God's sovereign action, they held that there was very little we ourselves could do. We could pray and believe God – that's all. And if we persevered in faith and lived long enough, we might well witness a worldwide outpouring of his Holy Spirit prior to Christ's return.

As much as I believe in God's sovereign love in sending both times of refreshing and a worldwide outpouring of his Spirit before the coming of the Lord, I also believe that we can do more than pray and trust.

For us, the bottom line on revival is our personal walk with God – and we can certainly do something about that. We can make choices and decisions that will bring about *personal* revival. And what happens within us can go on to have major effects in our homes and in society at large.

'Revive *me*, O Lord!'

The Word of God is clear: there are many things we can do, and must do, for ourselves.

Some will argue that because 'God can do anything', our personal spirituality, or lack of it, is no hindrance to his working. But they forget that God can only do what is consistent with his own nature. He can't, for instance, repent of sins, since he hasn't committed any. But we have, and the goodness of God leads us to repentance so that, when those sins are put away, he is able to move more freely in bringing revival.

A young Christian I once met was convicted by the Holy Spirit about not returning some lead that he had stolen from a roof in his pre-conversion days. For a long time he could find no peace of mind or heart.

'You know what the Holy Spirit is telling you to do, don't you,' I said.

'Yes, I need to return the lead and face the consequences.'

'Then do it. Until you do, no peace will be yours.'

He went back to the owner of the house with the lead he had stolen and told how he had come to Jesus Christ. The owner reacted in both amazement and pleasure. In the end, far from pouring recriminations on the young man, he shook him by the hand and wished him well.

From that day on, the young man experienced personal revival. He had needed to do what was *right,* and, having done it, he was revived. His story illustrates the psalmist's prayer: 'Revive me through thy *righteousness*' (Psalm 119:40 NASB). For many Christians today, this will be the way into personal revival and true peace.

Incidentally, for those who preach, this story is a reminder of the importance of including the need for restitution in our preaching of repentance.

Call to action

The psalmist also prayed, 'Revive me, O Lord, according to thy *word*' (Psalm 119:107 NASB).

As often as not, that word is a prodding of the Holy Spirit in the direction of personal change. He challenges us to straighten ourselves up in line with the written Word which he inspired.

Again, it is we who are responsible to act on his promptings. As the servant of Jesus, the Holy Spirit reminds us that the blood of Jesus Christ cleanses us from all sin (1 John 1:7). But the responsibility to confess and forsake those sins is ours. From the Word of God the cry goes out to readers deemed responsible: 'Cleanse your [own] hands . . .' (James 4:8 NASB); 'Rid yourselves of . . .' (Colossians 3:8); 'Hate what is evil' (Romans 12:9).

We dare not regard these exhortations as being of merely doctrinal or sentimental interest; they are given by the Holy Spirit for us to *act upon.* If our ways are offensive to God there is no way we can expect his blessing. Revival will elude us.

To the psalmist's question, 'Who may ascend the hill of the Lord?' comes the challenging answer: 'He who has clean hands and a pure heart' (Psalm 24:3-4). You can bring *yourself* to the place where personal revival can take place.

The Word says, 'Come near to God and he will come near to you' (James 4:8). Many Christians expect him to come near while they remain far off in conscious disobedience. But he won't. *You* have to make the first move – and, like slimming, nobody else can do it for you. Discipline yourself (1 Timothy 4:7 NASB). Revival will come when you act in line with the word of God to you.

Domestic revival

Revival may *begin* on a personal level, but it doesn't end there. God wants it also in the home.

Today, many a Christian marriage barely hangs together by a thread. Christian homes are rife with resentment, bitterness, silence and argument. Many of God's people are bringing up their children to believe that strife is normal and anger to be expected. At the same time they try to maintain a prayer life.

But the Word of God is abundantly clear: the husband must treat his wife with respect and love so that their prayers – including prayer for revival – will not be hindered (1 Peter 3:7). How many of *your* prayers have been hindered and unanswered because of a lack of forgiveness in your family relationships?

Domestic revival is sorely needed. It is time righteousness and peace came into our homes again. Love needs to be evident as at no other time.

Love and honesty

I was once getting ready to go to a prayer meeting, when my wife and I had a disagreement. I brusquely tried to exert my authority as head of the house and marched out of the door angry and frustrated. As I made my way to the prayer meeting I was in turmoil.

At the door of the church premises the Holy Spirit asked, 'Where are you going?'

'I'm going to pray.'

'Not before you've put things right with your wife.'

There was no point in arguing. He is always right. So I walked home, asked forgiveness of my wife and returned joyfully to the gathering of the believers.

Honest and loving relationships are a prerequisite for the blessing of God in domestic revival. Let it begin in your home. Listen to God and his Word, and act upon it. His firmness with you is only an expression of his love.

Pray with the psalmist, 'Revive me according to thy lovingkindness' (Psalm 119:88 NASB). Indeed, the fact that you have a relationship with God at all is because of his lovingkindness. Now he is wanting to take you further down the same road in your home life.

Possessed by possessions?

God wants us to live as people of the Way – people who do his will. A major hindrance to pursuing his will is a selfish attitude to *possessions*. Not that there is anything wrong in having things – as long as the things don't have you.

I was once visited by a friend who clearly needed a pair of shoes. Knowing that he took the same size as me, I went upstairs to get him a pair from my cupboard. As I came downstairs the Lord said to me, 'Who are these shoes for?'

'Lord,' I said, 'you know who they're for.'

'Your brother deserves something better than second-hand shoes,' he chided me. 'You need to give him those new ones that are still in the box.'

'But I only bought them last week, Lord,' I protested.

'Yes,' he replied, 'but they were not to be for you.'

I have learnt, and am still learning, that it is pointless arguing with the Lord. So I gave in, handed my friend the new shoes and found myself excited and thrilled when he gave testimony to the goodness of God. I was learning to emulate a God who is generous and kind in all his ways.

'Revive me in thy ways,' prayed the psalmist (Psalm 119:37 NASB). Learn God's ways. Find out from the Word what he is like and choose to imitate him (Ephesians 5:1). As you do so, you will find yourself being revived in his ways – especially in the realm of money and possessions. It is another choice you can make in the interests of revival.

No sitting back

All this serves to remind us that revival is very practical. Far from being a passive acknowledgement of God's sovereign power, revival as taught in the Word is an active pursuit of God, of his ways, his righteousness and his justice.

This is a truth we need to lay hold of today – not to sit back and wait for revival to happen, but to get actively engaged in provoking personal revival by taking heed to the commands of the Lord in his Word.

No-one can say he doesn't know what God wants. We will always find him if we seek him with all our heart (Deuteronomy 4:29). 'Anyone who comes to him must believe that he exists and that he rewards those who earnestly seek him' (Hebrews 11:6).

Therefore seek God. Seek him in prayer and in his Word. Listen to the promptings of his Spirit. Having heard his voice, obey him. Bring into line your relationship to himself, to others and to possessions.

Revival for you and me can come today if we will go back to these basics. As for revival on a national and international scale, that will follow in due time. First the acorn, then the oak. There cannot be the one without the other.

Let our prayer now be, 'Revive *me*, O Lord!'

Corporate preparation for revival

David Mansell

The biggest hindrance to revival is the church. Are we prepared to make the necessary changes?

The only thing standing in the way of world revival is a worldly church.

At the beginning, heathen darkness, Greek philosophy, Jewish ritual and demonic powers proved no match for a Spirit-filled church preaching Christ crucified and risen from the dead. Sin, sickness and demons fled at the name of Jesus. Thousands were added daily to the church.

It seemed that nothing could stop it. Persecution, prison and death, intended by Satan to quench the flame, only made it burn the brighter, as did the barrels of water poured over Elijah's altar on Mount Carmel. Soon, it seemed, the whole world would bow the knee and Jesus come again.

So what went wrong? Where was the Achilles' heel of this mighty church?

The menace within

'Keep watch over yourselves,' warned Paul. 'Even *from your*

own number men will arise and distort the truth in order to
draw away disciples after them' (Acts 20:28, 30). What Satan
could not achieve by persecution he achieved by infiltration
and corruption from within.

In came sect and schism under the guise of loyalty to super-
leaders. In came law and ritual masquerading as apostolic
tradition. In came acrobatic theological doctrines of special
wisdom that contrived to separate body and spirit in such
a way that a man could commit the foulest deeds without
it needing to trouble his conscience one bit. In came heretics
who denied even the sovereign Lord who bought them (2
Peter 2:1).

What was a dangerous threat in Paul's day is now the
norm. What was once the enemy to be defeated has become
the tradition to be defended!

Today the church stands silent, leaving it to a secular
'prophet', writing in the *Daily Express,* to draw the world's
attention to such appalling realities as a wishy-washy
Archbishop of Canterbury who firmly nails his colours to the
fence on every issue; an apostate Bishop of Durham who
denies the virgin birth of Christ and his bodily resurrection,
while telling us nobody can defrock him before he retires
because of the church constitution; and a bishop who in an
interview admitted his sexual preference for young boys,
whereupon the Archbishop did nothing but complain that
the matter had been made public.

Truly the Scripture is fulfilled: 'God's name is blasphemed
among the Gentiles because of you' (Romans 2:24).

Fundamental change

World revival cannot come without a fundamental shaking
of the entire church – Catholic, Anglican, Baptist, Methodist,
Pentecostal and, yes, all the 'new' churches, too. It has always
been the same: judgment must begin at the house of God
(1 Peter 4:17).

'Revival and change are almost synonymous terms,' observes Richard Roberts, 'and both clearly cut across traditionalism. There is no way revival can occur without major changes disrupting and reordering the life of the church.'[1] And we are not talking about making minor adjustments, admitting we are not perfect or calling a meeting where we declare our need for change. The change must be *fundamental,* just as it was when Jesus first came into the world.

Jesus' first step in bringing life to the world was to call for revival in the 'church' of his day.

First, he came to his own (John 1:11). First, he came to his temple as a refiner's fire and launderer's soap (Malachi 3:2-4). First, he confronted the moneychangers in the temple court (John 2:14-16). First, he publicly rebuked the leaders, denouncing them for their empty rituals, unbiblical traditions, hypocritical externalism and superstitious attitude to the fabric of the temple (Matthew 23).

Jesus did not work within the framework of traditional Judaism to slowly reform it. Nor did he wait quietly in the wings until the religious hierarchy were ready to make room for him on their stage. The time for revival had come. The time for repentance and restoration to pave the way for it. The time for the kingdom of God to come in power. A new superstructure on the old system would not do.

'You stiff-necked people, with uncircumcised hearts and ears!' thundered Stephen. 'You are just like your fathers: You always resist the Holy Spirit!' (Acts 7:51). The truth is, in every age the greatest opponent of the move of the Holy Spirit in revival has been the church.

Inbuilt opposition

Arthur Wallis has noted, 'He whom God chooses to be an instrument in revival may expect to be a continual target for Satan, who never seems to lack willing hands or legs to do his work, in the church as well as out of it.

'Many know of the contribution of Jonathan Edwards to

the New England Revival in the seventeen-hundreds; few know that he was ultimately compelled to resign from the church so signally blessed through his labours.

'Many know of William Burns, under whose ministry revival broke out in R.M. McCheyne's church in Dundee and elsewhere; few know of the gruelling he received in defending the work before a committee of his fellow-ministers. So it was with Finney and many others.'[2]

Of course, nobody actually *says*, 'Let's oppose the purpose of God and keep out the Holy Spirit.' But, assuming its denominations, institutions and traditions to have divine approval, the church defends them against all-comers, including God himself.

'Thank you, Lord, that we've been able to keep the doors of this place open for another year,' prayed brother Fred, just as he had done on every previous anniversary of my old church. True, the doors had been kept open, but not one person had come through them to find Christ. Meanwhile, we, the faithful few, had spent almost the entire year going through the life of David, with Fred contributing the same remarks every week!

God has a different view of this so-called 'maintaining the testimony' by powerless preaching to empty chairs: 'Oh, that one of you would shut the temple doors, so that you would not light useless fires on my altar! I am not pleased with you' (Malachi 1:10).

Jerusalem without God is Sodom and Egypt (Revelation 11:8). A church without the manifest presence of the Lord Jesus is no church at all, no matter what name it calls itself.

Reading *Foxe's Book of Martyrs*, one soon discovers the sad fact that much blood was spilt, not at the hands of infidels, but by the established church violently resisting the call for its own reformation. Happily, the fires of Smithfield burn no more, but one has only to give the establishment a prophetic poke to find that its love of tradition, rather than of the truth, still smoulders. Its embers are quick to burst into flame and dispose of any prophet bold enough to question its validity.

'If my people . . . '

'If my people, who are called by my name, will humble themselves and pray and seek my face and turn from their wicked ways, then will I hear from heaven and will forgive their sins and will heal their land' (2 Chronicles 7:14).

This is perhaps the most quoted verse of Scripture in relation to seeking God for revival. It clearly shows that revival is not only a sovereign act of God, but one in response to the preparation of the way by us, his people. 'The church can have revival when it will. Men greatly err if they are thinking to wait for God. God is waiting for men.'[3]

In reading the history of revival one discovers that in every case the breakthrough can be traced to the earnest seeking of God's face in prayer. What shall we do, then? Start a revival prayer group? Call the nation to prayer?

Humbling ourselves

First we must *humble ourselves*. Job had plenty to say for himself until the Lord showed up and asked a few questions. Then Job said, 'You asked, "Who is this that obscures my counsel without knowledge?" Surely I spoke of things I did not understand' (Job 42:3).

The humble heart is a listening heart. Like Samuel, it prays first to tell God that it wants to hear from him: 'Speak, Lord, for your servant is listening' (1 Samuel 3:9). Like Habakkuk, it invites God's rebuke: 'I will look to see what he will say to me, and what to answer when I am rebuked' (Habakkuk 2:1 margin).

In prayer, we need to use our ears before we open our mouth. Then, when our hearing moves us to cry to God, we will not pray the kind of prayer that proudly 'storms the throne', as if God can be pressed into pouring down his blessing by our simply praying round the clock.

No, the prayer that moves the hand of God comes from brokenness and humility. 'If my people will humble themselves' means that we will not ask the Lord, when he comes, to respect our prejudices and the church constitution or fit in with the order of service.

'To humble ourselves is . . . simply to take our rightful place before God . . . Are we willing to take that place? This is where breaking up the fallow ground begins. This is the first step, costly but indispensable, towards revival; and those unwilling to face it may as well cease to think or talk revival any more.'[4]

Prayer that does not spring from humility is arrogance, and goes unanswered. Humble prayer pleads with God to come and make everything exactly as he wants. It presents itself first in line for change. It hands the church back to its builder to check it out according to the plan, and then works with him till it truly is the habitation of God, filled with his glory.

Seeking God's face

Then we are to *seek God's face*. This means perseverance in our praying – praying through till God breaks in. It also means focus, asking him what practical steps need to be taken. If we are going to turn from our wicked ways, we must first know what they are.

Revival will not come through generally being sorry for our poor showing so far, generally confessing our faults, asking for God's blessing and then doing nothing in particular.

Just as Paul instructs the one who has been stealing to put his life right by stealing no longer and working for his living (Ephesians 4:28), we need equally specific instructions as to how we should put the church in order so that revival may come. Tozer, speaking on keys to revival, said, 'An honest man with an open Bible and a pad and pencil is sure to find out what's wrong with him.'[5]

Rubble removal

Revival always involves a clear-out.

Before the new could rise, Nehemiah had to clear away the rubble of city walls and temple which had lain desolate for seventy years (Nehemiah 4:10). True, it was rubble full of memories, but still rubble – to be cleared away, not treasured as sacred relics of a glorious past.

In the days of young King Josiah, the revival began with a total clear-out from God's house of all heathen altars, images and vessels. So zealous was he that he personally climbed on to the roof near the upper room of Ahaz, threw down the altars which had been built there, carted them away, smashed them to pieces and threw them into the brook Kidron (2 Kings 23:12)! Out, too, went the homosexual prostitutes, out went the idolatrous priests and out went all the mediums and spiritists (2 Kings 23:5, 7, 24).

It was this same zeal for the house of God that provoked Jesus to overturn the moneychangers' tables. In fact, it made the disciples think of the scripture that said, 'Zeal for your house will consume me' (John 2:17).

What will it take to bring world revival? It will take a zeal for God's house that will clear out everything that fails to express his own heart. It will take men of the Spirit – prophets – who have heard the commission: 'See, today I appoint you over nations and kingdoms to uproot and tear down, to destroy and overthrow, to build and to plant' (Jeremiah 1:10).

You want to build? Then there will be some pulling down to do first. You want to reach the world? Then put God's house in order!

Get rid of dead works

Dead works are works we do that God is not in and never asked for. Works with no moral value. Works that spring from religious strife and self-righteousness.

Paul describes them this way: 'Regulations . . . self-imposed worship . . . false humility . . . harsh treatment of the body, but they lack any value' (Colossians 2:23). We could include:

☐ Prayers proclaiming great desires after God which evaporate with the 'Amen'

☐ General confessions of fault that stop short of specific action for change

☐ Singing hymns that declare the greatness of God but expecting nothing great in my life or church

☐ Looking down on the brother wearing jeans while I feel I am honouring God by wearing my Sunday suit

☐ Religious furniture. The table may be called an altar and be dressed up to look like an altar, but it isn't an altar at all as there is 'no more sacrifice for sins for ever'

☐ Dressing up in religious vestments. They tell a lie by distinguishing between clergy and laity, while God does not

☐ Whispering and tiptoeing in meetings. If it is more holy to do this than to talk and walk normally, then let us do it all the time – in the office, in the street, round the house. If it is not holy in those places, let's not do it at all

☐ Plum-in-the-mouth praying. This means either that I am pretending to be pious, or that I really do have a plum in my mouth, in which case I need to finish it before I start to pray

☐ Holy days. Any activity that is not holy on a Sunday is not holy on any other day of the week

☐ Holy places. Getting baptised in the River Jordan imparts no more grace than getting baptised in the sea at

Southend. The only valid reason for using the Jordan
is if I live nearby

☐ Orders of service. Anything that will enable me to lead
the meeting even if God does not show up is a dead work,
whether it be printed in a book or handwritten on the
back of an envelope.

Tested by the Word

'Why is it that committed Christians who bow to the authority
of Scripture as far as their personal lives are concerned, have
often great difficulty in submitting to the same rule when
it comes to their church life?' asks Arthur Wallis.[6]

Jesus gives us the answer: 'You nullify the word of God
for the sake of your tradition' (Matthew 15:6).

Every revival has included the rediscovery of biblical truth
– truth which has challenged tradition. It was so in the days
of Josiah (2 Chronicles 34:14-15) and Ezra (Nehemiah 8:1-18).
It was so in the sixteenth century, whose Reformation was
born out of the rediscovery in Scripture of God's covenant
of grace and salvation by faith.

Revival will come when we put the Word of God in the
place currently occupied by our traditions, when we stop
viewing the Bible as an ideal for the church of the future and
act on it as God's command to us today. Constitutions,
traditions, beliefs and practices, be they ancient or modern,
must bow to the Word of God as the final and only authority
in all matters.

It was with this conviction that the Reformers lived and
died joyfully for the truth. 'Hellin Stirk, a Scottish woman,
when her husband came to the place of execution, said to
him, "Husband, rejoice, for we have lived together many
joyful days. But this day, in which we must die, ought to
be most joyful to us both, because we must have joy for ever.
Therefore I will not bid you good night for we shall suddenly
meet in the kingdom of heaven." '[7]

If men and women before us have paid the price in blood to hold to the truth of God's Word, will we not pay with our tradition and religion so that revival may sweep the world? Let's be specific:

☐ Infant baptism is a lie that has deceived many parents into believing that their child has become 'a member of Christ and an inheritor of the kingdom of heaven'.[8] It is by this unscriptural practice that the established church has for centuries dominated people's lives, claiming in this rite to hold the key to heaven

☐ Women elders and apostles may fit the current feminist trend, but the contrary is taught in God's Word. Does it matter? Anything that God saw fit to write is there to obey

☐ Because every truth is God's truth, to set it aside is to set God aside. Church government by vote, the separation of clerics and laity, state control, failure to discipline immoral practices within the church, the toleration of heresy, masonic ministers – all are chains which keep the church captive and must be broken

☐ Church membership by nominal profession rather than by new birth causes the church to be a mixture of believers and unbelievers, which immediately disqualifies it from being the house of God

Which will we set aside, tradition for truth, or truth for tradition?

If no denominations, what?

If we really believe that denominations are the will of God, why do we have so much discussion about unity?

In the midst of past revivals God has frequently obliterated denominational distinctions. That surely indicates that they are a hindrance to revival. Most Christians today agree that God will dispose of denominations; it is what we are to do with them now that poses a problem.

The issue is often wrongly stated as being simply, 'Should I stay in or come out? It is naive to think that leaving a mainline denomination to join one of the 'new' churches is the sure route to blessing. The real question is, 'Is the foundation Jesus only, or Jesus plus the constitution and tradition?' What makes a denomination is not variations in practice or label but having a foundation other than the practical lordship of Jesus.[9]

The church prepares for revival by preparing the way of the Lord, and that includes removing denominational attitudes and barriers:

☐ Do we do everything as followers of Christ, or some things as Anglicans, Baptists, Methodists or Pentecostals?

☐ Will we abandon sectarian tradition, dreams of denominational revival and all lesser loyalties for Christ?

☐ Do we have liberty to obey all the Word of God as part of the normal life of the church rather than have to do it in a corner?

☐ Is there room for every believer to function as a priest to God?

☐ Is the lordship of Christ practical in people's lives in a holy walk with God?

☐ Is there godly discipline in the church?

☐ Do we join the church by repentance, faith, baptism in water and baptism in the Holy Spirit, or by nominal adherence to the denomination and its traditions?

☐ Is there room for the Holy Spirit to speak and move in the gatherings, or is he excluded by the liturgy or the programme?

142 _Revive Us Again!_

☐ Is the leadership spiritual? Are we following men who are following Christ? Or is it a matter of labels and titles?

☐ Is the church governed by godly elders or by the common vote?

'The grand result to which revivals are . . . tending is the complete moral renovation of the world', wrote William Spragg.[10] Before the world can be touched, the church must change. If we will build our corporate life, like our personal life, on Jesus only, we will find we are all coming together; differences will die and revival will come.

What is the alternative? 'Because of his very nature, God cannot and will not permit spiritual decline to continue unchecked. He is ever halting and reversing the trend of the times by means of revival or judgment. Where his people are not prepared for the one, they shut themselves up to the other.'[11]

NOTES

1. _Revival,_ by Richard O. Roberts, Tyndale House Publishers, 1982
2. _In the Day of Thy Power,_ by Arthur Wallis, CLC, London, 1956
3. _Bringing in Revival,_ by G.E. Young
4. Arthur Wallis, op. cit.
5. Quoted in _Lord, Open the Heavens,_ by Stephen Olford
6. _The Radical Christian,_ by Arthur Wallis, Kingsway, Eastbourne, 1981
7. _A General Epistle to All Suffering Saints,_ from _Complete Works,_ by Thomas Brooks, Banner of Truth, London, 1980
8. _The Book of Common Prayer_
9. For a fuller treatment of this subject see _Stay or Move? – Church loyalty,_ by Tony Ling (with Karen Maheson), Harvestime, Bradford, 1989
10. _Lectures on Revivals of Religion,_ by William Spragg
11. _In the Day of Thy Power,_ by Arthur Wallis, CLC, London, 1956

Prayer with punch

Bryn Jones

We all agree that prayer for revival is vital. But do we actually pray? And if we do, are our prayers effective?

Prayer. We read books and articles on it. We hear dynamic messages about it. But the great challenge we Christians face is actually to get down and *do* it.

It's a fact that more people write or speak about prayer than pray, and even when they do pray, so much of that praying is ineffective.

Ineffective prayer

Prayer can be ineffective for a number of reasons.

The apostle Paul said, 'Pray in the Spirit on all occasions with all kinds of prayers and requests' (Ephesians 6:18). Prayer can be ineffective if we do not recognise that there are *different kinds of prayers* for different situations.

Second, Jesus warned against *praying from a wrong motive*, either preening ourselves as did the self-righteous man in the temple (Luke 18:9-14) or attempting to impress others with our religious sanctity as did the Pharisees on the street corners (Matthew 6:5-13).

James wrote about *prayer lacking the certainty of faith*, expressing instead a double-minded, unstable attitude (James 1:5-8).

Finally, there is *prayer without knowing God's will*, even while it is being made (see 1 John 5:14-15).

These categories alone nullify a lot of prayers.

Prayer principles

If our prayers for revival are to be effective we must pray in line with the principles outlined in God's Word:

1. According to his will

The basis of effective prayer is the knowledge of God's will (1 John 5:14-15). We need, therefore, to be assured that our prayer for revival is soundly based on Scripture.

An examination of the prophetic scriptures of the Old Testament, plus the combined teaching of the New Testament, assures us that God intends, before the return of Jesus Christ, to have:

- [ ] put down all his enemies (Acts 2:34-35)

- [ ] brought his people to maturity (Ephesians 4:11-13)

- [ ] perfected the church as a bride ready for his coming (Revelation 21:2)

- [ ] filled the church with his glory and power (Isaiah 60:1-3)

- [ ] reaped a rich harvest of lost souls (Matthew 9:37-38)

- [ ] made his church the most influential body of people on the face of the earth (Isaiah 2:2)

- [ ] fulfilled everything spoken by the prophets (Acts 3:21)

Nothing has taken place so far in church history large

enough in scope, powerful enough in impact, deep enough in effect or lasting enough in its consequences to claim that these and similar scripture promises have already been fulfilled. But because we know that this is God's will before Christ's return, we are stirred to pray for a visitation of God's Spirit on the scale necessary to fulfil these prophecies.

2. With burning hearts

James reminds us that 'the effective, *fervent* prayer of a righteous man avails much' (James 5:16 RAV).

Revival praying cannot be less than fervent if it is to be effective. It is just as impossible for a burning heart to pray a cold prayer as it is for a cold heart to pray a burning prayer. The praying heart must be gripped with a passion for God's purpose in order to pray with white-hot fervour.

Every spiritual awakening has been preceded by fervent prayer and has itself produced such praying. You cannot pray for revival in the same gentle, quietly grateful way you give thanks for a meal. It is a different kind of prayer, expressed in, and giving rise to, fervent, passionate cries from the heart.

3. With constant praise

All prayer, including prayer for revival, must be made in association with *thankfulness* (Ephesians 5:20).

We are not in despair, bleating to God; we are thankful believers calling on his name. We are not crushed by the powers of darkness; we have dominion over them and therefore boldly tear down their strongholds. We are not intimidated by our weaknesses but rejoice in grace sufficient for all our needs.

As we fervently pray for revival we can engage in singing high praises to God. At the same time we can loudly extol his virtues, magnify his name and rejoice in his love. These declarations in believing prayer provoke God in turn to manifest his presence, enthroned on the praises of his people

(Psalm 22:3 NASB) as the powers of darkness cower and flee from his presence.

4. With tears

Weeping is not a sign of weakness but of identification. Praying with tears for God's glory to be seen in his church identifies us with his own heart. To weep in prayer for lost and broken humanity identifies us with the heart of the 'great Shepherd of the sheep' (Hebrews 13:20).

General William Booth of the Salvation Army once received a despairing letter from a weary Christian 'soldier' working in India. Disappointed at the lack of response among the people after all his efforts, the man had despondently written to the Salvation Army headquarters in London to inform the General of the position.

Booth's reply was short and to the point: 'Try tears.'

Within a few months an elated Salvationist wrote from India about a moving of the Spirit of God which was bringing many to Christ.

In the great revival in Wales at the turn of the century it was noted that Evan Roberts, one of the principal leaders used at that time, would often not say a word in the meetings but simply lie on the floor groaning and weeping for the lost.

5. In the Holy Spirit

The great prayers of the New Testament, in their content, direction and effectiveness, show us men and women praying in the Holy Spirit (for example, Acts 4:23-31).

There are times when we cannot explain the difficulties experienced in prayer – why the heavens seem 'as brass', why we cannot feel the presence of God, why we battle with a tiredness that we didn't feel until we went to prayer. In such situations we have to learn to move beyond the natural, the visible, the circumstantial world around us, and enter the invisible realm within the veil, which we can do only by the Holy Spirit.

The natural mind often reaches the limits of our ability to pray. But we can discover a new freedom as the Holy Spirit within us intercedes in line with the will of God which, though unknown to us, is nevertheless perfectly known to him. Such praying becomes effective praying (Romans 8:26-27).

Praying in the Holy Spirit is not subject to factors such as time, place, circumstances or people. It is a matter of yielding ourselves to God's working within us – an experience that can only be described as being 'moved by the Holy Spirit'.

Often our natural mind objects to giving ourselves in this fashion and would seek to argue and rationalise the situation. Nevertheless, those who have learnt that it is 'in him we live and move and have our being' do not yield to the mind but train the mind to yield to the Spirit.

Praying in the Holy Spirit is the most effective form of prayer for revival.

6. With perseverance

How many times have we been engaged in prayer only to finally let go of our hope because the answer has been delayed? But the Bible teaches us that faith is the substance of things hoped for, the evidence of things as yet unseen (Hebrews 11:1).

To pray for revival we need to abide in God's promises, with our faith staying vibrant and strong, persevering in pursuit of that hope until it comes. Perseverance is a matter of confidently holding fast to God's promises. It means standing true to our conviction for revival, a revival rooted in the promises of his Word.

The Bible says, 'Against all hope, Abraham in hope believed' (Romans 4:18). Whatever happens to militate against the thing hoped for, we, too, need to continue believing. It doesn't matter if the political, economic or social conditions darken. We can remain confident that God will be faithful to his promise and pour out his Holy Spirit until the glory of God covers the earth 'as the waters cover the sea'.

'Though [the vision] tarries, wait for it; for it will certainly come, it will not delay' (Habakkuk 2:3 NASB).

Build dams!

David Matthew

A curious dream and its telling interpretation

Dreams are commonplace, but this one was extra vivid. The dreamer walked in a burning wilderness, his feet treading earth which was dry, rock-hard and devoid of vegetation, cracked open by the sun's merciless heat. The whole parched landscape cried out for water.

Then it came – a torrential downpour. In no time at all, signs of life appeared. Green shoots broke the surface. Seeds long dormant were being revived by the rain.

But, alas, the show of life was all too brief. The rain stopped, the searing sun reappeared and the earth again cracked open with drought. As for the seedlings, they shrivelled and died, and the dreamer found himself back in Scene One.

Where, he pondered, had all that rain gone? That deluge of thousands of tons of water which had fallen from the heavens – where was it now? Soaked into the earth. Evaporated. Gone. And with it, all that promising greenery.

It was then that the mysterious voice cried out, 'Build dams!' And with that the dreamer awoke.

Certain that this dream was of special significance, he recounted it to a fellow-believer, who explained its meaning. The souls of men, he said, are a barren wilderness. Society wilts for lack of the knowledge of God. From time to time, the Lord provides rain from heaven – outpourings of his Spirit in revival in which many come to new life. But, in time, the blessing fades and men again walk the dry earth of spiritual barrenness. The revival becomes just another chapter in the books on church history.

But dams *hold* water. And what's more, they release it in a controlled way, for the benefit of all. Thus it is, went on the interpreter, with spiritual outpourings. When that worldwide, end-time outpouring of the Spirit comes, God plans to have a multitude of dams ready to contain the blessing.

The dams are local churches. Not any old churches but ones structured on the divine pattern, marked by vigorous life, godly leadership, warm fellowship, evangelistic zeal, obedience to God's Word and spiritual alertness. The capacity for growth by subdivision is built in. Strong yet flexible, they do not depend on buildings, set forms of worship, traditions of men or trust deeds. Their only constitution is that of the New Testament.

Dam-building is hard work. It requires careful planning and concerted effort. Foundations must be dug deep. But how eternally worthwhile! What a joy, when the rain from heaven falls, to be able to hold on to it because we have prepared for it in advance! Such glad anticipation will keep us pressing on with the work in spite of the complaints of ecclesiastical conservationists.

Some men give themselves to bridge-building. Others build buttresses on to the failing structures of yesteryear. But restoration prepares the way for revival.

Anyone for building dams?[1]

NOTES

1. The true story on which this piece is based appears in *Times of Restoration*, by Orville Swindoll, Destiny Image, Shippensburg, 1983

Network your neighbourhood

Paul Smith

Practical steps in friendship evangelism to bring revival nearer

An overemphasis on God's sovereignty in revival can blind our eyes to certain facts at the human level. One of those facts – and a well documented one at that – is that most people come to faith in Christ through friends who are Christians. One study showed that seventy-nine per cent of the ten thousand Christians surveyed were born again through contact with Christian friends.[1]

There are practical implications for us here as we work towards revival and pray for its coming: pastors should encourage those in their churches to develop friendships with non-Christians in order to show them the love of God and introduce them to Jesus Christ.

Salt and light

Praise God that, in recent years, God's people have been coming out of the ghetto mentality and establishing contact with unbelievers without fear of becoming less holy. Thank

God that many churches are now giving their folk evenings
free to develop friendships, rather than cramming their weeks
full of church activities.

At the same time, many Christians are no longer looking
for fulfilment in serving God only in church responsibility
– preaching, prophesying, children's work, music and so
on – but finding their calling in society to be salt and light
for Jesus. It is wonderful, too, to see people full of the life
of God starting to face needy social issues, taking courses to
be better equipped to serve and rolling up their sleeves for
grass-roots involvement.

As we do good to all people, God will open up the way
for sharing the specifics of the gospel with at least some of
them.

Networks of friends

One beneficial exercise is to ask Christians to identify their
networks of friendships by writing down the names of people
they know fairly closely – in their family, at work, in the
neighbourhood and socially. Many will be surprised to see
how many people they know and can influence for God.

By meeting in small groups, Christians can then pray about
their contacts with specific individuals and implement plans
for reaching their neighbourhood.

Friendship is not only the most effective means of winning
people to the Lord, it is also the key to seeing them added
to the local church and continuing to follow the Lord. Willard
Black states that ninety per cent of new members will stay
in their congregation if:

1. They can articulate their faith

2. They belong to a smaller subgroup

3. They have four to eight friendships in the congregation

To be added to the church means to be added to people.

We must make newcomers feel welcome and care for their needs so that God can truly join people to people.

None of this is intended as a substitute for the sovereignty of God in regeneration and sanctification. It is simply an acknowledgement of the fact that, in his sovereignty, he chooses to work very largely through personal contacts.

Get moving

The mobilisation of the local church is the key to winning the world. God is bringing his people out of the spectator syndrome, where witnessing and miracles are performed only by the full-time professionals or their close circle of co-leaders. Replacing this 'us and them' mentality ('We church members are the ones with the problems – they're the ones with the answers') is the realisation that the whole church is to operate together as a team to reach the world.

Even a small church has a total combined network of contacts that is staggeringly large and that can be exploited for God. 'Warm contact' evangelism is the best. But there are some areas, towns and cities which we will never reach with the gospel through existing networks of contacts. In these places there is a need for deliberate pioneering.

Ray Bakke, co-ordinator of the Lausanne Committee on urban evangelism, writes, 'In the next seven seconds thirty-one babies will be born. Half of these babies will end up living in cities.'[2]

Established Christians can choose to uproot and move, under apostolic direction, to a new town or city. They must be clear in their minds that friendship is the key to winning people to Christ. They will then view every contact with new neighbours, work colleagues and shop assistants as a means of winning people to themselves, first of all, in order then to introduce them to Christ.

Programmed evangelism (as opposed to spontaneous friendship evangelism) into these towns and cities is essential if we are ever to reach the world. It needs to be geared towards breaking into the complex existing networks, where the knock-on effect can take place. Word gets round!

Bridge of friendship

Having advanced into a totally new area, my own church recently turned 'cold start' evangelism into a bridge of friendship by delivering a leaflet depicting a cartoon character and a message that we wanted advice from local people on how we could best serve the community. We returned in person a week later to collect ideas and to share our faith when appropriate.

This non-threatening approach distinguished us from other religious door-knockers and softened people's hearts towards us. We kept simple records and revisited the warmest contacts, some of whom have since come to faith in Christ and been added to us.

It is important in door-to-door work to remember that we are not out to argue or persuade at every house, but to find those in whom God is already at work by his Spirit.

We took up the most frequent suggestion – that we should do something for children during school holidays. Play-dough, dressing-up, face painting, collage, etc., on the local green attracted many children and parents, and gave us a profile as Christians not out just to 'save souls' but to befriend people and bring the love of God to their whole life.

Since then we have been exploring and developing other strategies – mother-and-toddler group, kids' club, specific interest groups for young people, a pregnancy advisory service and visitation of the elderly. We are using any means which gives us meaningful interaction with non-Christians so that they are touched by the life of God in us.

Some people can only be reached in their homes. Over the last few months we have had the joy of helping several senior citizens find Christ, some of whom were frightened to go out of their homes much. Now that they regularly meet with the church, many express appreciation for the love, trust and security they feel among us.

Filling the gap

As well as taking the initiative in networking our neighbourhoods, we need also to network the existing structures in society:

☐ to become known to social services, medical professionals, police and teachers as trustworthy people who care

☐ to find and fill the gaps in provision for different sections of the community – old people, single parents, the poor

☐ to know our communities better than anyone else, our availability giving us credibility for the advance of the gospel

No-one pretends that this is revival, but it is one means of preparing for it. As we explore different ways to increase our sphere of influence, we move in the general direction of revival, when we will see the whole world touched with the good news of Jesus Christ.

NOTES

1.   Study carried out by the Institute of Church Growth, Pasadena, 1981
2.   Quoted from *The Urban Christian*, Marc Europe, 1987

Gideon's progress

Terry Virgo

*The triumph of Israel under Gideon at the battle of Midian
furnishes clues to the triumph of the church*

Can we be anything but revival optimists when God has
promised that the increase of the government of Christ will
have no end?

The government will rest on his shoulders and the people
who previously walked in darkness will see a great light. These
are clear biblical statements of the determined purpose of God
concerning his Son and they will certainly come to pass –
but how?

An Old Testament clue

Isaiah is the one who prophesies these events and he sheds
further light when he says that it will come about *as at the
battle of Midian* (Isaiah 9:4 NASB). That is the battle
associated in most of our minds with Gideon. Somehow that
particular battle (see Judges 6 – 7) sums up some of the
features of the ultimate triumph of Christ's kingdom.

The Israelites, in a time of national decline, were at the

mercy of the all-conquering Midianites, whose countless war-camels constituted a powerful new tactical force. They suddenly swept into the area and devastated the crops and flocks of the Israelites, who were forced to dwell in caves and dens, a pathetic shadow of their former selves.

Under Joshua they had been an invincible army but that was all in the past. They were now a spent force, of no significance in their generation.

Communist camels?

Can you see this tragic picture as reminiscent of the church as she is seen in Britain and many other countries today? The church is regarded as an irrelevant relic of a bygone era, useful for adding colour to national events like coronations and royal weddings but, in terms of real life, of no significance to modern man. A far cry from revival!

Some Bible commentators have argued that the Israelites were defeated by Midian because they had never encountered camel warfare before. Certainly it posed a new problem for which they had no answer from previous experience. Similarly, some argue that today's church has never before encountered the combined forces of television, atheistic humanism, eastern religion, materialism and communism.

'We live in a difficult age' is the forlorn cry. Some would even have us concentrate all our prayers on the destruction of these modern evils, as though that could solve all our problems.

A closer look at the Scriptures, however, leaves us in no doubt about the real source of the Israelites' plight. The camels need have been no more a problem than the Red Sea or the walls of Jericho if only Israel had been walking in obedience and faith. No, their enemies prevailed over them not because of superior weaponry but *because God was no longer with them.*

God was, in fact, strengthening their enemies against them.

Such was frequently the case in the Old Testament. Why should we consider it impossible in the New? Indeed, the book of Revelation shows churches threatened with closure, not because of the forces of the world or the devil, but because the risen, glorious Lord of the churches was himself challenging their right to exist.

God isn't scared

The first lesson of the battle of Midian is that *God is absolutely sovereign.* He is not perplexed about how to keep up with the twentieth century and the curiosity of modern man. He is not fearful that his gospel is too simplistic for modern scientific enquiry. He reigns, a King supreme!

God's enemies never pose a threat, but his people will only enjoy his blessing and see victory when they are obedient and believing. Our own problem as we seek revival lies not in the power of our enemies, real though it be, but in the lack of God's blessing in our churches.

Instinctively, the Israelites began to sense the reality of the situation and to cry to the Lord in their distress. God in his mercy heard them and sent a prophet to tell them the cause of their failure: They had compromised and served the gods of their neighbours.

God will never bless compromise. Tragically, many who speak and sing about their allegiance to King Jesus also bow the knee to the modern gods of materialism, sexual uncleanness, human wisdom and man-made religion.

God's response to Israel's cry was to call for a revival of whole-hearted commitment to himself. At the same time he began his first moves towards a mighty battle to rout Midian.

Too strong to use?

The initial move was an extraordinary interview between the angel of the Lord and a cowardly young man named Gideon,

whom God was pleased to call a 'mighty warrior' (Judges
6:11-24). It was the biggest joke since God had called the
childless Abraham 'father of a multitude'!

Surely, if God was about to restore Joshua-style victories
to Israel he needed an outstanding young man for the task,
especially after all those years of decline and defeat.
Amazingly, he searches out a weak, insignificant youth.

Here, then, is the next vital lesson for us: *Those factors which
we see as disqualifications are the very qualities God is seeking!*
God chooses not many wise, not many mighty, not many
noble. Instead, he goes for the foolish, the weak, the base,
the despised and even the things that are not, to bring to
naught the things that are. No-one is too weak for God. Sadly,
many are too strong.

Gideon did have one positive qualification, one which
always attracts God's heart like an open flower draws the bee:
he was *thirsty for God*. He had a longing for God's power to
be seen. He yearned for a revival of Israel's glory under God's
blessing.

This young man was heartbroken with what had become
the norm. A generation had arisen which did not know God
and had never seen his mighty works, and these were the
people dictating Israel's expectations.

But Gideon had no confidence in the theory that miracles
concluded with Joshua and were merely intended to be
instrumental in the early invasion of the land. He believed
in an unchanging God of limitless power. To him it was a
cause of deep frustration that God was for them, yet there
was so little sign of his power. Why were they not seeing
mighty miracles, signs and wonders?

I trust that we also have abandoned the teaching that the
supernatural was only for the early church, something to
inaugurate its initial thrust. I trust, too, that we are not
complacent in the naive belief that our experience of
charismatic life so far is a full demonstration of the purpose
of God for our day. It is not!

Longing becomes believing

Though he looked so feeble, Gideon had a heart crying out for God's glory. God's standing promise is to pour water on him who is thirsty and floods on the dry ground. Are we, though weak and feeble like Gideon, also, like him, thirsty for God? Do we deplore the lack of mighty demonstrations of his power?

God will come to thirsty people to satisfy their longings. But to really use them he must turn their longings into genuine *faith*. He never despises weakness but he will never bless unbelief. Gideon became a man of faith. That great list of faith-heroes in Hebrews 11 includes Gideon who 'by faith . . . from weakness [was] made strong, became mighty in war, put foreign armies to flight' (v32-33 NASB).

Gideon came to have *confidence in his calling*. God had called him and met with him, and though he was slow to believe, he ultimately came to a place of great confidence, with resulting victory.

God wants leaders who have no confidence in the flesh but a genuine and growing confidence in the Lord who called them. Pleading weakness after God had called him earned Moses a severe rebuke from God. It does not matter how weak a man is, provided he is genuinely called. If God has sent him to do a job he is invincible until it is done.

Key tactics

Two further steps of preparation were needed before Gideon was ready.

First, he had to apply the word of the prophet to his own personal life. The altar to Baal in his own home had to be torn down. There is no point in our rejoicing in the general prophetic word about revival to come unless we respond with specific obedience in our own lives. Revival begins in the individual heart. Leaders and people alike are called to single-minded devotion to Christ, without which we cannot be his disciples.

God rewarded Gideon's obedience by clothing him with the Holy Spirit's power – the second step of preparation – thus equipping him for the coming battle. The prayers of Israel were answered, then, first by a *prophetic word* and then by a *new anointed leadership*, a pattern to be repeated in the stories of Samuel, David, John the Baptist and the Lord Jesus.

But there is a third phase of God's plan to consider, namely, the *gathered, committed army*. This key tactic was also used by David and Jesus. In considering it, let us remember that God has declared this to be the way the kingdom will ultimately come to triumph.

A committed army

Much has been said about the selection of Gideon's army. Preachers have speculated wildly about the significance of those who lapped the water and those who did not. I want instead to concentrate on the more obvious features of the story, ones often overlooked.

For a start, they were a *fearless* army. When the fearful had been invited to go home the brave remained for the battle.

The end-time battle, too, is going to call for great courage. Some have already suffered great opposition and character-assassination in the battle, but this has so far been almost exclusively at the hands of their Christian brothers and sisters who have felt it right to oppose certain new developments in the church.

The battle will get rougher when the *world* begins to feel the impact of our growth and blessing. They will fight without observing any rules and we will see the sort of injustice that Paul and the early believers encountered from the vested interests of their day.

They were also an army *willing to express their obedience to God by obeying the leader God had given them.*

Individualism is one of the great enemies of God's purpose in gathering any army. It is often piously cloaked by, 'I don't feel led' or, 'The Lord hasn't told me yet.' So we continue to run our private lives in the kingdom of God.

This army was willing to be subdivided at Gideon's direction, without cries of, 'I prefer it when we are all together' or, 'I want to be in Gideon's group'! They were happy to leave Gideon to lead, confident in his anointed leadership. Great release comes to the church of God when this principle of spiritual authority is accepted and leaders appointed by God are given freedom to lead.

Such leaders must, of course, prove themselves worthy of being followed by being men of action as well as word. They must be willing to lead from the front and not simply whip others into action by harsh preaching.

Gideon demonstrated such leadership when he shouted, 'Look at me and do likewise!' The car-bumper sticker 'Don't follow me, follow Jesus' is not the motto of the leader after God's heart.

One of the vital factors in God's programme for the end-time triumph of the kingdom of Christ is the resurgence of genuine, responsible, charismatic leadership followed by a committed army full of faith and obedience. When that is true, revival will not be far behind.

Spiritual weapons

The weapons used in Gideon's battle have also presented preachers with a glorious opportunity for sanctified imagination. The lamps, trumpets and pitchers have all been interpreted in various ways.

Certainly they were of no tangible value whatsoever in natural warfare. Gideon's army was totally outnumbered and their victory depended entirely on the correct use of *spiritual* weapons, portrayed in the lamps, pitchers and trumpets.

The first weapon they used was *unity*. The individual

responsibility of breaking the pitchers was only of real worth
in the battle if everybody acted together. An occasional splash
of light on the hillside followed by irregular trumpet blasts
would have had no great effect on the enormous Midianite
army. Victory was totally dependent on the army's acting
as one man.

Jesus prayed that we would all be one so that the world
would believe. God commands the blessing where unity is
top priority.

Unity is a great spiritual weapon whose power has yet to
be unleashed. Local churches must strive for one heart and
mind, not as a forlorn hope but as a clearly obtainable goal.
So must national and international Christian leaders.

God has said, 'It shall be as at the battle of Midian', and
on that day Gideon's army moved with absolute unity, even
when separated in the darkness. God will have such an army
to bring in revival blessing in these last days.

Not only did they move with unity but also *each was working
properly in his right place*. There was a wholehearted commitment to the matter in hand. No-one was distracted or out
of position.

The mature church of the last days will demonstrate that,
though all are in their place, they will not act identically but
with a glorious variety of gifts and callings. All will be for
the common good. Unity of purpose will be expressed through
great diversity of gifts.

Strategy plus dependence

Israel's extraordinary triumph came out of a vital com-
bination: *a definite strategy plus total dependence on God*.
Without God's miraculous intervention the army would have
been discovered as the totally inadequate force it actually was.
Nevertheless, there was a plan.

It was at the middle watch that Gideon's alarm was sounded
– when some Midianite soldiers were returning from sentry

duty and others were replacing them, so that armed soldiers were moving among the sleeping troops.

To the Midianites' dismay it appeared that they had already been invaded because troops, represented by lights and trumpets, appeared to surround them on all sides. God then inspired a panic which led to a complete rout.

In seeking revival we must note this balance of human strategy and dependence on God. We often swing to one emphasis or the other. Either we put all our eggs in the basket of church growth, goal-setting and human achievement or we give ourselves totally to prayer and waiting for heaven-sent revival, despising all human endeavour. The pattern set at the battle of Midian shows us how to bring these together, resulting in total victory.

Thus Isaiah portrays for us the sure triumph of Christ's kingdom. Light will burst on those in the darkness. The increase of his government will have no end. It will be as at the battle of Midian, that sample of total defeat transformed into glorious victory.

To us a child is born. To us a Son is given. Let us obey him, follow the pattern and see his kingdom come.

Be a revival rebel!

Paul Smith

If we are serious about revival, we will not be afraid to rock the boat

One day during the bus boycott in Montgomery, Alabama, a white man approached Martin Luther King Jr.

'For all these years we've been such a peaceful community,' he said. 'We've had so much harmony in race relations. And then you people started this movement and boycott. It has done so much to disturb race relations. We just don't love the Negro the way we used to, because you've destroyed the harmony and peace in race relations that we once enjoyed.'

'Sir,' Martin Luther King replied, 'you've never had real peace in Montgomery. You've had a sort of negative peace in which the Negro too often accepted his state of subordination. But this isn't true peace. True peace isn't merely the absence of tension; it is the presence of justice. The tension we see in Montgomery today is the necessary tension that comes when the oppressed rise up and start to move towards a permanent, positive peace.'[1]

Despite many setbacks and much personal cost, Martin Luther King was successful in changing the status quo which so comprehensively denied the freedom promised and legislated by Abraham Lincoln a hundred years before.

Today, with the scent of revival in the air, prophets and prophetic communities of God's people are similarly accused of upsetting the religious status quo. Many are the tactics used to try to persuade the prophet to be less radical, more accommodating, in his vision for a pure bride of Christ. Where this approach fails the prophet is marginalised, in the hope that 'if we ignore him, perhaps he'll go away'.

But prophets, and the communities they inspire, will not go away, nor merge into the background. They take the need for revival seriously. They have been gripped with a vision and would rather die than settle for less than God's best.

They see the tension they create as necessary to change the lukewarm state of Christianity today. As a result, they are accused of failing to love the body of Christ, when in truth their actions arise entirely out of love.

'The greatest victory of this period,' wrote Martin Luther King, 'was that we armed ourselves with dignity and self-respect. We straightened our backs up. And a man can't ride your back unless it's bent.'

God's spokesmen today are refusing to settle for mixed churches where regenerate and unregenerate share membership; churches which are lukewarm; churches whose meetings are predictable, be the tradition old or new; or churches in which believers are oppressed and defeated. They fight for freedom and justice, for a people called to enjoy their birthright inheritance in Christ, for churches strong enough to contain the flood-waters of revival when it comes.

As with Hezekiah, the Lord is with them as they rebel (see 2 Kings 18:5-7).

NOTES

1.   Quoted in the biography of Martin Luther King, *Let the Trumpet Sound*, by Stephen Oates, Search Press

A better kind of revival

Wesley Richards

Four Christian leaders discuss their deep convictions about the coming revival and its implications for today's church

Everybody's talking about revival these days. But we keep coming back to the question: What do we mean by the term? And how can we work towards seeing it come in our generation?

For some answers I turned to four men with a prophetic ministry, all at the forefront of preaching, teaching and church-planting: Tony Ling, Bryn Jones, Alan Scotland and David Mansell.

We needed at least an attempt at a definition to start with. So, 'What,' I asked, '*is* revival?'

'Some see it as a way of stopping redundant church buildings being sold off as warehouses,' replied Bryn Jones. 'Others see it as a shot in the arm for existing church life. Others again see it merely as multitudes being brought to faith in Christ. But revival in New Testament terms is a season of

refreshing preceding Christ's return, a visitation of God that
will spell change for the church.'

I invited him to be more specific.

'Revival must contribute to restoration,' he explained, 'which
in turn will lead to the return of Christ [Acts 3:21]. Any
revival that fails to help restore the church to God's ideal
– and that means change – is mere revivalism. It will leave
us with the need for yet another revival in a few years' time.'

Perhaps he needed to define 'restoration', I suggested.

'Restoration in the Bible sense isn't restoring something to
its original condition, but bringing things to their ultimate
fulness,' Bryn Jones replied. 'It's not a return to the problem-
ridden New Testament church but an advance to the fulness
of Christ, expressed in the whole body of Christ without
schism, spot or blemish, touching this world just as Jesus
did two thousand years ago.'

   'Scripture is clear,' added Tony Ling, that God is heading
for a pure, mature church, a unity of faith. Every revival must
therefore serve that ultimate purpose. In revival God intends
to hasten what would otherwise take generations to achieve.'

**How, I asked, was this distinct from a reformation of
existing church structures?**

David Mansell rose to this one. 'Revival,' he said, 'isn't God
coming to validate what we are, approving our denominations,
brightening up our services or making us feel holier. Revival
is God coming to his church to do what *he* wants to do. Unless
we welcome him without reserve, revival will not go beyond
the superficial.'

   'I agree,' added Bryn Jones. 'Revival can hardly be God
coming to validate what we are; it's because of what we are
that we're crying for revival!'

Why, I wondered, had previous revivals come and gone?

'Because people have tried to own the revival, to contain it within their denominational boundaries,' said David Mansell, 'or because they've tried to exclude what God has introduced. Outbreaks of spiritual gifts, miracles and visions, for example, because they didn't fit in with a denomination's previous history, have been discouraged, causing the revival to fade.'

'Why did Judaism miss the visitation of God in Jesus' time?' asked Bryn Jones. 'Because it was entrenched in a religious pattern that could no longer bend to the purpose of God. It has been the same in revivals ever since.'

'*Re*vival,' commented Tony Ling, 'means bringing back to life what had life before. Any dead church will have introduced practices that are impossible to revive because they've never known the life of God. He won't revive the accoutrements of men.

'How, for instance, can unbiblical practices like infant baptism and nominal Christianity based on assent to a creed be revived? They can't. And when men are determined to see revival touch things that have never had life, what little life does exist among them will soon die.'

I was curious as to *why* the religious establishment hadn't welcomed revival as it should.

Bryn Jones explained: 'Let's take a couple of examples. Wesley found himself in conflict with the established church of his time because he wouldn't recognise parish boundaries in the preaching of the gospel. The colliers of Evan Roberts' day were put out of the chapels because of the sobbing, the breaking and the healing miracles that took place.

'This parallels what Scripture records about the visitation of God in Christ two thousand years ago: The people "did not recognise the time of God's coming" to them [Luke 19:44]. Why not? Because the religious power structure was threatened by the man of Galilee. The liberated life he lived threatened their religiosity.

'Some of us will recall that the mid-fifties saw a significant wave of prayer for revival in this nation. Cottage groups everywhere were praying for it. I'll never forget a Welsh lady in her eighties who spoke to me at one such meeting.

' "Bryn, don't make my mistake," she said. "Years ago I was in a cottage prayer meeting, praying for revival, when we heard that the revival party with Evan Roberts had come from Lacher to Aberdare and were in the chapel. I went up there. It was very early in the morning and all the lights were on but I could hardly get through the door because of the crush.

' "What I saw horrified me. I saw some men and women lying on the floor weeping. Then there were some colliers standing on the pews in their working boots, waving handkerchiefs in the air and shouting, 'Hallelujah!' Some people were singing, some were praying, some were shouting, some were sobbing – all at the same time. I said to myself, 'This is total disorder,' and went home.

' "When I arrived, I said to my sister and my mother, 'We must pray that God will save us from this deception that has come among us, because God only does things decently and in order.'

' "It was two years later," she went on sadly, "when the revival was over, that I realised that the very thing I'd prayed for had come and gone – and I'd missed it."

'Her tragic story has stayed with me. God isn't necessarily coming to do what we think he should do, but if we're truly praying for revival we must say, "God, come and do what *you* want to do." '

'What about today?' I asked. 'What aspects of revival would threaten the present religious establishment?'

Bryn Jones was clear: 'For a start,' he said, 'I believe the visitation of God in our time will take Christianity out of ecclesiastical premises into the market-place of life. Sunday services in special buildings will give way to seven-days-a-week life expressed wherever people live, with the breaking of bread at any time and in any place. That offends religious people for whom only "ordained" men can "administer the sacrament". How do you set up your altar and candles in the street?

'Also, the rediscovery of the priestly ministry of *every* believer threatens the pension, job and status of religious professionals.'

Wasn't it true, I asked, that virtually every past revival had left behind another denomination? Wouldn't a future revival inevitably do the same?

Tony Ling agreed that it had often happened. 'But it's not inevitable,' he assured me. 'It has happened mainly because a group of people have wanted to embrace the new revelation that God has brought, while many others have refused it. God intends revelation for the whole body, but it has been embraced fully only by some, who have then been forced into isolation by the rest. The Pentecostal revival early this century is a case in point.'

David Mansell added: 'If, when God moves in revival, some people withdraw and others embrace it, you have a division. But who caused it – those who moved with God or those who drew back?

'It's always those who withdraw from the moving of God who cause division. In fact, in reaction to revival, you often find the old thing more entrenched than before. But it's always quick to pin the accusation of "dividing the body" on those who move in the mainstream of God's purpose.'

If godly people had failed to move with the Spirit in past revivals, why, I wondered, shouldn't people today miss it for the same reasons?

'I think some *will* miss it,' said Tony Ling. 'There'll always be those who are too late, too lazy or just don't want to know. But in the end God will have what he has always desired – one church, a pure church, his people.'

Bryn Jones pointed out that 'possible' and 'inevitable' were not the same. 'The next wave *could* end up as in the past,' he said, 'but to say it's inevitable is to make history god and God subject to history. By saying that a day is coming when the church will reach maturity ready for the return of the King, God has served notice on history that it will not inevitably repeat itself.'

'One reason why revival declines,' observed Alan Scotland, 'is because people see it merely as a phenomenon or impersonal manifestation of power. They forget that it's a visitation of God himself by the Holy Spirit. He comes, as always, to have personal dealings with people, opening up their inner lives. Some Christians find that hard to cope with and withdraw to safe traditional ground.'

I commented that these 'personal dealings' had often included such phenomena as falling down, loud weeping and crying out. This had provoked strong criticism from some. Would it still be a stumbling-block in the future?

'Most likely,' replied Alan Scotland. 'As we've already heard, critics of the Welsh revival of 1904-5 wrote it off as emotionalism. But God clearly owned it by bringing about great changes for good in the whole of society. There will always be some who fear and criticise. When God turns up in person, they don't like it.'

David Mansell added: 'In revival, God wants to come for habitation, not just visitation. Some don't mind God coming for a while, provided he goes when he's done as much as they want him to do. But when he says, "Look, I'd like to stay and finish the job. I'd like to tackle the things you *haven't* prayed about – your traditions, your practices and prejudices, your authority structures, your control of meetings and your unreadiness to give room to the Holy Spirit,'' then people begin to react and say, ''We only asked you as a visitor.'' '

'Visitation and habitation are two facets of revival,' explained Bryn Jones. 'A visitation is a season of refreshing. Habitation is what it should lead to — restoration. That's why successive revivals have been necessary: people wanted the visitation but didn't like the idea of God's staying on. People wanted revival but not restoration.'

Many people today were praying for revival, I commented. How could they pray effectively?

Bryn Jones didn't hesitate: 'The only prayer that brings response is the prayer of faith,' he declared, 'and faith comes by hearing the Word of God. We must base our expectation of revival on God's Word.

'It's not enough to pray because the need demands it, because the church is in a mess, because there are more lost people than ever, because Islam is getting stronger or because we're being invaded by alien religions. None of that produces faith. We must root our praying in the Word of God.'

'We must also action what we're praying,' said David Mansell. 'It's the height of unreality, for instance, to pray, ''O God, forgive us for our divisions'' and then stay in our denominations. Where possible, we must be the answer to our own prayers.'

So what specifically should we be doing today?

'Where men know they have wronged their brethren they need to go and see them and be reconciled,' said Bryn Jones. 'Instead of talking about our brother, we must go and see him personally.

'Then there are personal things. If, for example, you have mental battles with unclean thinking and are watching wrong movies and videos, or reading wrong newspapers, then what is needed is not revival but a change in your viewing practices. Prayer is no substitute for obedience.'

'Repentance is a key,' said Tony Ling. 'And repentance isn't always forsaking the bad for the good; sometimes it's forsaking the good for the best. It's a constant willingness to change – and that means, not prayer, but action now.'

Alan Scotland added: 'Obedience is part of the *humbling* that prepares the way for revival. To humble ourselves means being honest about the issues at stake and not camouflaging them with religious talk. As a group of men we are discovering right now what this means, as God puts his finger on things that need to change.'

When I asked for personal examples, the men were disarmingly frank.

Bryn Jones mentioned a tendency to compromise his convictions by placating people who were satisfied with less than the pursuit of God's full purpose. Tony Ling specified a proneness to be intimidated by other people and the desire to be well thought of. David Mansell highlighted the wish always to get his own way and to manipulate people and circumstances to bring it about.

All the men spoke of repentance for these weaknesses and a moving into wholeness. Clearly they were practising what they preached!

In their times of prayer together for revival, the men had wept profusely. I wondered what tears had to do with preparing the way?

'Tears are an expression of deep feeling,' said David Mansell. 'They often mean identification. You may weep if you identify with someone's joy or sorrow in a film. In the same way, when you identify with God in his feelings, in his love and his grace towards yourself or towards the world, tears just come.'

Bryn Jones remarked that tears had always been a part of his deep experiences with God. 'I'm sometimes astonished at the groanings and tears I go through in waiting on God,' he said. 'I feel it is God taking our eyes through which to weep, just as he takes our lips through which to pray.'

Tony Ling saw tears as a hallmark of those who carry the burden of God, like the ancient prophets. 'They groaned and wept,' he said, 'because they were being touched by the feelings of God. I think God is looking for a people who can identify that way today.'

He described his own weeping as 'beyond emotion'. It wasn't even the result of a build-up within himself. 'Something will trigger it and the tears will flow, my heart will ache and my spirit will groan,' he explained. 'It's an expression of travail – what I imagine birth-pangs must be like.'

Alan Scotland said his tears flowed as a result of entering into something of God's own perception of the state of the church and the world. 'I think how precious people are to God, and how desperately they need him,' he said. 'I think how far removed we are from where we ought to be as a church. I ache for us all to enter into the fulness of God.

'My tears sometimes replace words. I'm speechless, but my tears are saying something and sowing something that I believe will be reaped in God.'

What, I asked, were they looking to see in a future and maybe final revival that had not been seen in past revivals?

'That Christ will be given his rightful place at the head of not only church affairs but world affairs,' answered Alan Scotland. 'I'm looking for the restoration of all things, everything being handed over to Christ so that he in turn can hand them over to Father.'

'A revival that spreads and spreads,' said David Mansell, 'with wave after wave not hindered by man, not blocked by

tradition, not opposed by prejudice. I look to see every wave
of the Spirit embraced and welcomed, so that as he comes
and is welcomed again and again, the visitation will become
a habitation. Then I look to see Jesus coming and sealing
that with his personal return.'

'The people of God enjoying the manifest presence of God
among them,' was Bryn Jones' reply. 'We will then see
miracles, healing and salvation as the norm – great joy and
great fellowship, without the division of religious labels or
religious boxes. We'll all own Christ as supreme, express
Christ as the centre of our fellowship, declare Christ as the
essence of our gospel, and the whole church will be a God-
filled people of rejoicing.'

Tony Ling agreed. 'Not the production of another
denomination, nor even the containment of existing
denominations, but a flood of God that will sweep them all
away. When Jesus died he removed the middle wall of
partition. The only walls between men and women are the
ones they have built themselves. I look to see a move of the
Spirit of God that will remove them.'

**Clearly they were expecting a pure church on earth. But
did most evangelical and charismatic Christians believe
that?**

'No, they don't,' Tony Ling assured me, 'but the Bible
teaches it. Jesus prayed that the unity of the church would
be the ultimate testimony to the world of who he was.
Therefore it has to come on earth.'

Bryn Jones added: 'The World Council of Churches, the
Evangelical Alliance, ecumenical organisations and ministers'
fraternals all indicate that Christians know they are meant
to be one. Those are external efforts to express a unity that
isn't really there. It won't come about through those things,
but come about it will. Christ's prayer can't remain
unanswered.'

One charismatic leader, I pointed out, had recently stated that he loved denominations because they expressed the diversity of the church – a diversity out of which he believed unity would come.

Bryn Jones disagreed. 'Historically, denominations aren't diversity, they're tragedy,' he asserted. 'They're evidences, not of the difference in God, but of the differences between men. Many of them are the product of personality clashes, not of revelation. How can something born of discord express the unity-heart of God?

'Paul described the divisions in Corinth as carnal. Let's be honest: Many Christians place their denominational loyalty above their loyalty to the brotherhood of Christ as a whole. True, there are godly people in every denomination, but as the body of Christ comes to maturity it must drop everything that hinders the expression of its unity.'

David Mansell was equally adamant, calling the statement 'an utter insult to God'. And it was unscriptural, too: 'The early Christians were one in heart and mind [Acts 4:32]. Church divisions today aren't to do with varieties of expression of the heart of Christ – many of them express unscriptural standpoints, historical divisions and people falling out with one another. They call for repentance, not rejoicing, and are a hindrance to revival.'

'If denominations are so good, the more we have, the better,' said Tony Ling. 'But if they're wrong, we need to get rid of them all. We must go either for more – or for none. I believe we must go for the zero option.'

Some Christians, I observed, believed that we will all be one in heaven, but never on earth.

'That view isn't tenable,' said David Mansell. 'If our divisions are going to disappear when Jesus comes, how can they be so good now? And if they aren't so good now, why don't we ditch them right away? I'm sure some professing Christians will always remain denominationalised, but the Word of God leads us to believe that the dominant thing at the end will be a pure church marked by victory and unity.'

If the coming revival would produce a pure church, what, I wondered, would it do for the world at large?

David Mansell foresaw the victorious church presenting Christ to a needy world. As a result, 'people will be convicted of sin at their workplaces and in the streets,' he said. 'This has always been a mark of revival. Evangelisation won't just be in meetings; it will be the presence of God everywhere, touching the whole world. Nations that have been totally closed to the gospel will find God breaking in on them supernaturally.'

And would that include countries dominated by Islam and animism?

'Most certainly. Christ will overcome all opposition. I once met a brother from Surinam. He'd been a witchdoctor and the leader of a group of spiritists – all of whom had come to Christ. No missionary was involved. One day this fellow had had a vision of a man who said, "I am Jesus," and told him what to do.

'When a missionary came in years later, it was to find that they knew whole passages of the Word of God. They knew about Jesus and the New Testament church. When God himself opens the heart, it will break, however hard it has been.'

Bryn Jones added: 'The whole world will be impacted by a supernatural gospel through a dynamic Christian community. Everything will be affected, including politics, the environment, economic policies, social programmes and attitudes to the developing nations.'

Would this impact on the world at large, I asked, be a right-wing, Moral Majority-type effect?

'Evangelicalism has become too aligned with conservative policy and right-wing fundamentalism,' he replied, 'much to the pain and loss – and death, in many cases – of thousands in the third world. We must get out of this syndrome.

'Through revival, righteousness and justice will be the order of the day, and we will be apolitical. Social blights will be removed. There will be no racism, no treading on the poor, no extortionate interest rates that keep them in their poverty. The Christian community will be so large and powerful that it will produce a wholesome society.'

I pointed out that evangelicals had always been associated with prayer for revival. Would they, I wondered, be in the flow of future revival or constitute an obstacle to it?

Bryn Jones was forthright: 'Generally speaking, the evangelical mind is too narrow. God made clear in the covenant with Abraham that he was intent on blessing the whole world. But evangelicals have tended to feel that anybody who does not subscribe fully to their position is beyond the pale of fellowship and unable to be used by God.

'But God is bigger than the evangelical camp. People outside it are not beyond the blessing of God. He can, and will, bless anybody – and use them, too. Some evangelicals won't accept the gifts of the Spirit, but that won't stop God giving and using those gifts. Other evangelicals, who do practise the gifts, can't believe that God will use anybody who doesn't. But God will use whoever he wills.'

'Evangelicals tend to have their doctrines buttoned down too tight,' commented Tony Ling. 'God won't be confined that way. They tend to be preconditioned in their thinking as to what the revival will be, how it will happen and what it will produce. I doubt if it will fit their pattern, so they'll have a major problem.'

'In my experience,' said David Mansell, 'most evangelicals don't think beyond seeing the lost won to Christ. That constitutes an obstacle to revival, because there's more to it than that, namely, the bringing in of the kingdom of God. And that means personal holiness, it means Jesus coming to me, to my attitudes and motivations, to my family, to my relationships, to the church, to the nations, to the world.

'Unless our revival expectation embraces these deeper issues, unless it affects behaviour, unless it means meetings become true meetings with God, unless it provokes a dismantling of clerical hierarchies, unless it affects society, politics and economics, we can't claim it to be the fulfilment of the promise to Abraham that "in you all the nations of the earth will be blessed".

'So while we don't equate the coming of the kingdom with some economic development or other, neither do we equate it with people getting born again but continuing in a mess, unbaptised, unfilled with the Holy Spirit, still slaves to addictions, failing with their families and unaware of what's going on in the world.

'We're looking for a revival that starts in a person's innermost being and then reaches to the uttermost parts of the earth and touches every aspect of human life. Then, and only then, will our precious Lord return.'

Contributors

Roger Aubrey is pastor of City Church, Cardiff, South Glamorgan. Before entering full-time ministry in 1985 he was group manager for a youth training company. He is married to Dianne and they have two young children.

Ivor Hopkins, formerly a missionary in the Caribbean and Guyana, now leads Wirral Christian Fellowship, Merseyside. He and his wife, Clarine, have six children.

Bryn Jones is a well known Christian speaker and teacher based in the Leicester area. He leads Covenant Ministries and travels widely to preach throughout the UK and elsewhere. He is the author of *Worship: A heart for God, According to Your Faith* and *Effective Prayer* (Harvestime). He and his wife, Edna, have four children.

Keri Jones has a recognised apostolic ministry exercised in churches within England and Wales. He and his wife, Carol, have five children.

David Lazell is a self-employed Christian researcher and writer based in Loughborough, Leicestershire. He has a history degree and is particularly interested in the history of religious journalism. He is currently working on a new biography of evangelist Gypsy Smith.

Tony Ling has a wide preaching and prophetic ministry. He is the author of *Stay or Move? – Church loyalty* (Harvestime). He lives in Keighley, West Yorkshire, with his wife, Hazel, and their two teenage sons.

David Mansell has a prophetic ministry and lives in Chigwell, Essex. He and his wife, Christine, have two grown-up children.

David Matthew is a Christian teacher and writer based in Bradford, West Yorkshire. He is the editor of *Restoration* magazine and the author of several books, including *Dead Dreams Can Live!, A Sound Mind, The Covenant Meal* and *Belonging* (Harvestime). He and his wife, Faith, have three children.

Wesley Richards is pastor of King's Church, Windsor, Berkshire. He is also involved in the oversight of Slough Christian Centre and Centro Rey, Madrid, Spain. He and his wife, Carol, have three young children.

Alan Scotland leads New Life Christian Fellowship, Loughton, Essex. He also travels widely, particularly in South Africa, teaching the Word of God. He and his wife, Betty, have four children.

Paul Smith is pastor of Living Word Community Church, Basildon, Essex. A former policeman and school-teacher, he is married to Grace and they have three children.

Hugh Thompson has a prophetic/teaching ministry and leads Calderdale Community Church, Halifax, West Yorkshire. He is the author of *Essential Foundations, Go and Make Disciples* and *Be Eager to Prophesy* (Harvestime) and, with his wife, Rosemary, *Fulfilment in Marriage* and *Successful Parenthood* (Harvestime). They have four grown-up children.

Terry Virgo is based at Clarendon Church, Brighton, Sussex. He leads the New Frontiers International team, which plants and serves churches in the UK and other countries. He is the author of *Restoration in the Church* and *Men of Destiny* (Kingsway) as well as *Praying the Lord's Prayer* and *Enjoying God's Grace* (Word). He and his wife, Wendy, have five children.

The late **Arthur Wallis,** who died in 1988, was a popular speaker and writer with a heart for revival. His books included *In the Day of Thy Power* (CLC), *God's Chosen Fast, Pray in the Spirit, Into Battle, The Radical Christian* and *China Miracle* (Kingsway). He is survived by his wife, Eileen.

THE BEST IN CHRISTIAN READING

Other good books from Harvestime:

From the Prophet's Pen

Insights of a man of God
by Arthur Wallis

These selected writings express the godly wisdom of the prophet who penned them — the late Arthur Wallis, a man committed to seeing revival.

Some would consider him as more a teacher than a prophet. He was indeed committed to Scripture and loved to expound it as a stimulus to Christian living. But it was his insistence on its 'here and now' relevance, its right to shape our personal and church life today, that moved him over the borderline from teacher to prophet.

That prophet, though dead, still speaks. And his writing carries the flavour of personal godliness to which fellow-leaders have paid tribute:

'A godly man, a judicious leader and a loyal and fair friend'
— *Ern Baxter*

'The deposit of his life in Christ has changed us. His effect will go on and on and, as a result of his life and ministry, we will be spurred on, too' — *Tony Morton*

'Arthur has contributed much. His influence will remain through the many lives he touched and through his writings'
— *Campbell McAlpine*

ISBN 0 947714 75 8   £4.95

Other good books from Harvestime:

Apostles Today

edited by David Matthew

Few topics are of greater interest today. Questions abound: Didn't apostleship die out with the Twelve? Or, if there are apostles today, how do we recognise them? Is an apostle the apex of a pyramid of authority? What about apostolic teams — how are they formed and how do they operate?

This compilation of writings by a variety of authors — including the late Arthur Wallis — tackle these and related questions. Many of the writers are recognised as apostles by a growing number of Christians in Britain today.

ISBN 0 947714 58 8   £3.25

These books are available from leading Christian bookstores.